"Lucie Hemmen has created her most useful tool yet in *The Teen Girl's Survival Journal*. In a time when teen girls are under more pressure than ever, this engaging resource provides a space for teens to learn about themselves, express themselves, and adopt new skills and habits that make them stronger. I can't think of better timing."

—**Jesse Burgess, LMFT**, former clinical manager for Youth Services in Santa Cruz, CA

"*The Teen Girl's Survival Journal* is cleverly designed to help teen girls build mental health habits, while also getting to know themselves more deeply. With its fun layout, this journal is a place for teens to self-reflect and express themselves, while also learning new skills and practices that make them more resilient. I will definitely recommend this journal to the teens in my practice and in my life!"

—**Tom Western**, licensed marriage and family therapist with over thirty years of experience

"Teen girls will enjoy this fun and creative journaling experience that guides them in adopting healthy habits they can take into adulthood. Lucie Hemmen creates an informative and engaging experience designed to cultivate important skills that serve mental health. A must-have for today's teen that I will certainly recommend."

—**Kristin Baron, LMFT**, certified IFS psychotherapist and consultant

"*The Teen Girl's Survival Journal* is a delightful guide full of important information for those who want to take charge and make a change in their mental health. It provides a safe space to learn, reflect, and explore one's inner self."

—**Isabel Maddahi, AMFT & AT**, primary therapist

T0271497

THE
TEEN
Girl's
SURVIVAL
JOURNAL

your space to learn, reflect, explore &
take charge of your mental health

LUCIE HEMMEN, PHD

Instant Help Books
An Imprint of New Harbinger Publications, Inc.

CONTENTS

WELCOME

Welcome to your mental health journal. As a psychologist specializing in teen girls, I created this experience especially for you. Over the years, I've seen thousands of teen girls in therapy and noticed big changes in pressures they face. While it's never been easy to be your age, it's more complicated now than ever—and mental health is taking a hit.

The good news is that teen girls are also resilient! Teens are often natural "psychologists." You have the capacity for keen insight into yourself and other people. You probably think deeply (or even overthink!) and grasp mental health concepts quickly with support and guidance.

That's where this journal comes in. It's a balance of learning, reflecting, and exploring yourself to protect and elevate your best mental health. It is habit-based, because the more solid, healthy habits you collect and practice, the better mental health you create for yourself. Even better, your brain rewires for the new habits you practice—and so does your nervous system!

That means that as you swap out not-great mental health habits for good ones, you'll improve yourself at a structural level. Better yet, you will feel your best and enjoy life more. *Yes!*

HOW TO USE THIS JOURNAL

I recommend you progress through your journal front to back. Moving sequentially allows habits to build on each other and make the most sense.

There are eleven chapters guiding you to:

 LEARN a brief psychological concept to build your psychological intelligence, so you can...

 REFLECT on how it applies to you. Unlike obsessing, ruminating, and overthinking, healthy reflection is the practice of thinking deeply to understand and grow. You need to know yourself to grow yourself. Once you've reflected, you'll move on to...

 EXPLORE how it feels to interact with what you're learning, so concepts become personal and relevant. From there, you will...

 ELEVATE your mental health by bringing new concepts into your life, where they count! Elevate sections offer creative ideas and practices you'll have ready to go when you need them.

To keep things fun, and to pack in as many ideas and strategies as possible, you'll find smaller sections along the way, including challenges, psych tips, soul soothers, and more.

Some prompts contain multiple questions, so if one doesn't grab you, another will. Just go with whatever prompt speaks to you or ignore all options and write what you want to. This is your space. Make it work for you!

Recommended materials:

- Colored pens/pencils and crayons
- A quiet space
- A soothing or refreshing beverage

NOTE OF ENCOURAGEMENT:
If you come to a section or prompt that feels emotionally overwhelming, use your best judgment and either seek more support or skip it entirely. Good support options are often family, therapists, school counselors, teachers, or other adults who are emotionally safe.

CHAPTER 1

Warm Up

> **"**
> You can't stop the waves, but
> you can learn to surf.
> —Jon Kabat-Zinn
> **"**

> **"**
> Life keeps happening.
> I just handle it better.
> —Elsa, age seventeen
> **"**

 # LEARN

As you may know, teen mental health problems are on the rise. If you haven't had struggles yourself, you probably know someone, or several people, who have had them. Potential reasons include: busy schedules and the pressure to succeed, social media use that may entertain you but leaves you feeling worse (and behind on your homework), a lack of mental-health coping skills, a lack of healthy habits, a lack of sleep, social stress, family stress, a lack of supportive resources, and worry about the future.

What you may not know is that mental health, like physical health, is something you can build, strengthen, and protect. It's not something you either have or don't have. In reality, *most people* will face a mental health challenge at some time in their life. Like physical health, mental health can fluctuate throughout life. Your mental health is greatly affected by your mental health habits and ability to cope with the stresses you face.

 # REFLECT

Take a minute to reflect on your personal mental health in the past year. On the scale below, place a heart to represent where you see yourself along the continuum.

In the past year, I've felt:

not great.	like a roller-	mostly good
I've had	coaster of ups	and able
a hard time.	and downs.	to cope.

If you placed your heart to the left or in the middle, keep in mind that struggling is not uncommon. You face a lot of internal changes and stressors as well as a lot of external stressors in your life. This journal is here to help you.

If you placed your heart to the right, great! Know that there's always more to learn. Just like your physical health, mental health gets stronger and more consistent when tended to regularly.

 **EXPLORE**

How about your current mental health habits? Most people have a mixture of healthy and not so healthy. Healthy habits include caring for your nervous system, journaling, regular exercise, good nutrition and hydration, good sleep, time in nature, time with good people and/or pets, kindness and compassion, and a balanced lifestyle.

Not-so-healthy habits include numbing and distraction (drugs/alcohol/scrolling/screens), avoidance and procrastination, perfectionism and busyness, rages and meltdowns, shutting down and withdrawing, self-harm behaviors, impulsive acts, and risky behaviors.

Choose one healthy and one not-so-healthy habit to explore. Feel free to choose something from your own life that hasn't been mentioned here.

NOT-SO-HEALTHY HABIT: _____

Your experience with this habit (when it started and what it offers you, even if you know it's not the healthiest):

_____

_____

_____

_____

How it makes you feel and how it affects you/your life/others:

_____

_____

GOOD HABIT:

Your experience with this habit:

How it makes you feel and how it affects you/your life/others:

 **ELEVATE**

Good job, you're working on yourself already. No matter what your habits are now, adding more healthy ones is the key to feeling your best. Experiencing ups and downs in your mental health is human. Getting through those ups and downs largely depends upon your mental health habits. Here's your first one: *practicing affirmations*.

 Affirmations are simple sentences designed to teach your brain to focus on what you want.

Directing your focus *intentionally* allows you to "unstick" from negative thoughts that crush your mood and confidence. Affirmations are also helpful for overthinking because they slow and calm an anxious mind. Unlike false positivity, which denies true feelings, you'll learn to accept *all* your feelings, *while taking charge of your focus*. Affirmations organize your focus in a healthy, hopeful, positive, and encouraging way.

To add affirmations as your first mental health habit, give the following ones a try and make sure to notice how each one feels. Read each affirmation out loud, before closing your eyes and repeating it silently. In the first reading, you'll absorb the content intellectually. In the second reading, you'll absorb the content emotionally. (Intellectual processing happens in your head. Emotional processing happens in your body, where all your feelings live.)

Repeat the process for each affirmation. Here goes:

- ✦ *I open my heart and my mind to healing and growing.*
- ✦ *I'm ready to embrace this journaling experience.*
- ✦ *I believe I can feel better.*
- ✦ *I believe I can feel more confident.*
- ✦ *I can do hard things.*
- ✦ *I can make big changes.*
- ✦ *The only person fully responsible for my mental health is me.*

Now it's your turn to write an affirmation for yourself. Just take a moment and tap into what you'd like to create for yourself. Trust what comes to you.

Choose an affirmation that is best for you—that you most want to create as your reality. Write it three times in the space provided here. Use some different colors or vary your handwriting style to involve your creative mind. Notice the extra layer of processing that happens when you (a) write and (b) incorporate a splash of creativity.

Ready for your first challenge? Here it is.

 ## *Challenge*: PRACTICE AFFIRMATIONS

Okay, you're exploring a new habit already. Now for the real challenge: making it stick. As you consistently practice new mental health habits, you'll find that they become more than what you *do*—they're who you *are*. They will become part of your identity—the way you see yourself—and your confidence will grow as a result. It will eventually feel weird *not* to practice your healthy habits. Until then, here's your first challenge to get you going:

Write one or more affirmations on a piece of paper, a sticky note, or your phone, where you can easily refer to it throughout the day. Tailor your affirmations to exactly the place or places you most need support. If you've been feeling socially anxious, your affirmation might be *I feel friendly and confident toward everyone I see today.* If you're feeling tired and unfocused, your affirmation might be *I'm generating all the energy I need to focus and feel good today.* Every day when you wake up, let your affirmation be your first thought of the day. Check in with that affirmation throughout the day, whenever you can, because you're working on absorbing it fully. As you do, check in with your body and notice how you feel when you direct your thoughts and feelings with care and intention.

Great job! You just completed your mental health warm-up.

Now time for a psych tip that is as quick as it is effective!

NOTE OF ENCOURAGEMENT:
If you notice resistance to deeply embracing these thoughts, be patient with yourself. You may have some negative thinking habits that don't want to budge. Thinking more supportively will improve with time and practice.

PSYCH TIP: FIVE-MINUTE BRAIN DUMP

You know that satisfying feeling of taking everything in your backpack or purse and dumping it out? This tip is a lot like that, only you'll be decluttering your brain instead of your backpack. It involves the simple act of dumping the contents of your mind onto paper. From your to-do list to something annoying in your day, all content is welcome. The act of dumping the clutter helps you clear space and quiet a noisy mind, so you can feel calmer. For this exercise, no grammar, penmanship, punctuation, or spelling accuracy is required. Inner critics are strictly forbidden!

Before starting your brain dump, take a deep breath to get a sense of the thoughts, feelings, or *noise* inside your head or body. The only materials required are you, your thoughts and feelings, a place to dump them—and five minutes. You can just dump your thoughts or grab-and-go from the prompt warehouse here:

- What was the highlight of your day?
- What was the most frustrating thing that happened?
- Who are you annoyed at, and why?
- What worries do people have about you that are unwarranted?
- What worries don't they have that maybe they should?
- What situations triggered big feelings today?
- What do you keep inside that you want to share?
- What's in your life that you'd like removed?
- What isn't in your life that you'd like added?
- How are you holding yourself back in life?

- What person in your life do you depend on the most, and why?
- What do you need to let go of, and why?
- What is your funniest quirk and when did it start?
- What or who frustrates you the most?
- Who has hurt you, and how did you respond?
- What mistake keeps repeating in your life that you'd like to resolve?
- What parts of your personality do you love the most?
- What do you hide and why?
- What do you love about life?
- What does your ideal day look like?
- Where do you want to direct your energy?

Ready, check the time, and then GO!

What was that like for you? Share anything you noticed:

Some teens say they don't really *know* what's in their internal clutter until they start writing. As they get into the flow, more and more tumbles out. Did you notice that, and if so, how did it feel?

NOTE OF ENCOURAGEMENT:

If self-expression is hard for you, this may be a tip that requires patience. You may be used to keeping your thoughts and feelings to yourself and struggle to find the words to express yourself. It may take time for you to feel more comfortable, so be patient as you grow in this new way. Come back to this tip any time you're stressed and overwhelmed.

Also, this is *your space*, so always feel free to modify an exercise to make it perfect for you. If you like a ten-minute brain dump, grab some extra paper and do it! If two minutes works better for you, trust yourself. After your dump session, follow up with a little self-care like a healthy snack, a big glass of water, or the soul soother you're about to learn.

Now that your mind is less cluttered, you're ready for a nice soul soother. A brain dump is one of many *top-down* mental health practices that work with your mind to calm your nervous system.

This soul soother is a *bottom-up* approach that focuses on your nervous system directly. By focusing on your body, bottom-up approaches are a perfect go-to when calming your mind feels impossible.

～～ SOUL SOOTHER: WALKING MEDITATION

This practice is based on the fact that when you move your body slowly and take charge of your focus, your nervous system calms. When it comes to strengthening your mental health, you'll be collecting *lots* of different ways to care for yourself.

When you think of meditation, you probably picture a person seated upright on the floor with their legs crossed—very lotusy and maybe a little intimidating or unappealing. The walking meditation accomplishes the same goal only without needing to sit still. It's been around as long as sitting meditation but is less well known. It's an excellent soul soother that requires nothing beyond you and somewhere safe to walk. While walking up and down a quiet path in nature is ideal, you can do a walking meditation in an airport if you want to. It'll just be noisier.

This walking meditation is a teen favorite.

WALKING MEDITATION

Choose a path or area that's safe. To begin, clear your mind with a long deep breath and big body stretch. As you exhale your deep breath, try to make the exhale a little longer than your inhale. Imagine your focus dropping from your head into your body and, slowly but surely, down into your feet. There's no right or wrong way to imagine. Just explore and trust yourself.

Imagine your feet taking the rest of your body for a nice, slow walk. Then…

1. **STAY FOCUSED ON YOUR EXPERIENCE OF MOVEMENT AND SENSATIONS.** Walk slowly, as if the only important thing in the world were your experience of walking. Notice everything possible about the feeling of each foot lifting, stepping, and the shifting of weight, as if you were going to write a precise explanation of the process for someone who's never done it. Focus your eyes in front of you and slightly down, so as not to get distracted by visual inputs. Narrate the pattern of your feet silently: right foot, left foot, right foot, left foot.

2. **INTEGRATE YOUR BREATH.** Now, add in an awareness of your breathing. Breathing through your nose (if you can), notice the air moving in and out as your feet continue to carry you forward. Make small adjustments in your posture or arm swing, as desired. When your mind wanders, come back into your body and the experience of movement.

3. **BRING YOUR MIND BACK.** Thoughts will, of course, sneak in to distract you. No problem, just notice and silently name the thought (*distraction*), without following the content (*I've got to text Tessa about Friday*). Patiently, and continually, refocus on your physical experience and the sensation of walking slowly.

   When you feel complete, acknowledge yourself with appreciation and notice how you feel.

   Do you have five or ten minutes now? Give it a try.

NOTES ABOUT MY EXPERIENCE: After you finish your walk, use this space to write about it.

NOTE OF ENCOURAGEMENT: Next time you feel anxious or stressed, give this ancient meditative practice a try. When you move your body slowly and mindfully, your nervous system gets the message that you're safe, which turns down your anxiety dial and turns up feelings of well-being. This way, you are directly working on your own nervous system to calm down. Working with your focus (by bringing your mind back on track again and again) builds and sharpens your ability to focus in other aspects of your life too.

Focus is like a muscle that you build through practices like this! Who doesn't want to focus better?! Healthy habits build you into your best self, and this is an example of one habit creating multiple benefits.

You're stacking up powerful mental health habits already. When you explore a habit you especially like, make a note of it in the back of this journal where you'll find a "Favorites" page.

CHAPTER 2

Grow Kindness

> It takes courage to be kind.
> —Maya Angelou

> I'm learning to be as kind to
> myself as I am to my friends.
> —Emma, age sixteen

 **LEARN**

Ever notice how easily annoyed you feel when you're tired or stressed? Whenever you feel low, irritable, anxious, tired, or stressed, it's *much* harder to be kind and compassionate with yourself and with others. Being hard on yourself and others is a normal response to stress. It's just not likely to make you feel better, because while you may vent frustration, you're also creating more negativity (and potentially alienating the people you need the most).

Here's where kindness comes in, and while it might seem like a lightweight mental health habit, it's actually *the foundation of all other habits*. Opening your heart to yourself is essential, because you can't grow or work on yourself when you are your own worst enemy. You just can't.

Teen girls who stay stuck in self-criticism and self-hatred have a hard time elevating their mental health and happiness. It's okay if you don't feel warm and fuzzy when you're struggling. But when you *choose* kind behaviors (toward yourself and others), you *create* better feelings. In other words, don't wait to feel positive feelings before you choose kind behaviors—kind behaviors create better feelings.

 **REFLECT**

When it comes to kindness, how do you see yourself? Place a heart to represent where you are on the scales below.

Kindness toward others:

Definitely
not on my
radar.

I'm hit
or miss.

I'm strong
in this area.

Kindness toward self:

⭐——————————————⭐——————————————⭐

I'm my own
worst enemy.

Not horrible,
not great.

Yes, this is
a strength
for me.

How do you feel about where you are on each scale? If you slide to the right, what benefits do you see for yourself? For your relationships?

_____

_____

_____

_____

_____

_____

_____

_____

♥

NOTE OF ENCOURAGEMENT:
Many teens report that when they feel good, kindness is easy and natural, but when they feel bad, it's impossible. Focusing on action instead of upsetting thoughts and feelings can help you free yourself from *stuckness*. Kind action + pausing to feel good about it = a powerful step in the right direction.

 **EXPLORE**

If you prioritize being kind to yourself for one week, **what negative habits would you need to remove?** Dig deep and identify any and every habit, large or small, that works against you.

What would you add? Fill this page with as many ideas as you can. Feel free to think small, because small acts are often more realistic; plus they build momentum in the right direction and add up.

Since what you focus on *gets bigger*, let's focus even more on the power of kindness.

Exploring kindness in your relationships, fill in the following boxes:

The people in my life who show me the most kindness...	Acts of kindess I've received...	A moment of receiving kindness that pops into my mind...
The people in my life I show the most kindness to...	I show people kindness by...	A moment of giving kindness that pops into my mind...

 NOTE OF ENCOURAGEMENT: Reflecting deeply on happy moments is called *savoring*. It's an excellent mental health habit that positively affects your brain and your mood. Savoring can be a lifesaver when you're in a negative thinking spiral that's keeping you awake at night. Next time you find your brain treacherously combing through the details of the day (looking for what you did wrong), forcefully change the channel, choose a good memory, and practice savoring yourself to sleep. You can't control every thought that comes into your mind, but you *can* choose what to focus on!

 **ELEVATE**

To elevate kindness as a mental health habit, let's pair an activity you've known since childhood—coloring—with a breathing exercise that stokes kind feelings. Start by taking a deep breath into the feeling of kindness. (Again, you're using your focus to encourage a desired feeling.)

As you connect to the feeling and invite it to linger, explore this three-step Heart Breathing practice:

1. **INHALE:** Imagine breathing warmth and kindness into your heart.
2. **EXHALE:** Imagine releasing any stress or pain your heart is holding.
3. **REPEAT** as many cycles as you feel like.

When you've got the hang of Heart Breathing, use crayons or other coloring tools to extend the emotional state you've created. Coloring is meditative in that it reduces the thoughts of a restless mind as it calms your nervous system.

This exercise integrates different strategies and modalities to encourage feelings of calm.

NOTE OF ENCOURAGEMENT: Breathing exercises are not fluffy woo-woo. They are a scientifically backed way to calm your nervous system. When you focus on slow, deep breathing (making your exhales longer than your inhales), you turn down your body's stress response and turn *up* your body's calming response. Even better, the more you do them, the better your nervous system gets at switching from stressed to calm. The payoff increases over time because you're actually resculpting your nervous system!

Challenge: RECORD ACTS OF KINDNESS

Use this space to record kind acts for the next three days. Make sure to offer at least one kind gesture toward another and toward yourself (beyond what you'd typically do) every day. If you feel resistance to acts of kindness with family, no need for guilt. Becoming independent is part of teen development, and it often manifests as feeling annoyed at parents and siblings. Most teens find that if they push through that resistance, the effort is worth it. As you practice your acts of kindness, notice how they affect your mood and your feelings about yourself and others.

 Day 1: _____

ACT OF KINDNESS TOWARD ANOTHER: _____

HOW IT FELT: _____

_____

_____

ACT OF KINDNESS TOWARD SELF: _____

HOW IT FELT: _____

_____

◎ Day 2:

ACT OF KINDNESS TOWARD ANOTHER:

HOW IT FELT:

ACT OF KINDNESS TOWARD SELF:

HOW IT FELT:

◎ Day 3:

ACT OF KINDNESS TOWARD ANOTHER:

HOW IT FELT:

ACT OF KINDNESS TOWARD SELF:

HOW IT FELT:

Wrap-up: You're doing great! Don't forget to add your favorite new habits to your list at the end of the journal!

 **PSYCH TIP: TETHERING**

Tethering is a psych trick that helps you stick to a new habit by connecting this new habit with something you already do. For example, since you go to school already, you can tether heart breathing to your ride or walk to school. If you take a shower every morning (or evening), you can tether heart breathing to your shower. The possibilities are endless.

More ideas:

- You can tether an act of kindness to dinner time by saying something positive about the meal or by offering to help.

- You can tether affirmations to folding your laundry or walking the dog.

- You can tether coloring to your nighttime routine and savoring to going to sleep; both will soothe your mind as a healthy swap away from mindless scrolling.

What form of tethering do you want to explore?

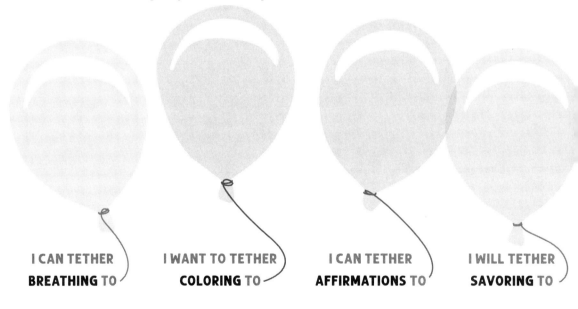

**I CAN TETHER
BREATHING TO**

**I WANT TO TETHER
COLORING TO**

**I CAN TETHER
AFFIRMATIONS TO**

**I WILL TETHER
SAVORING TO**

Excellent! You're stacking up new mental health habits. Transfer tethering to your favorites list if you especially like it.

≋ SOUL SOOTHER: THE HO'OPONOPONO

Part of being a teen is the experience of intense, often inconvenient and very uncomfortable, emotions. Angry outbursts can feel like they pop out of you, alarming other people and even yourself. You may feel guilt mixed with a stubborn resistance to apologize. This is not uncommon!

Many girls feel defensive about their less-than-kind moments, not because they don't care but because they actually *do* care and just don't feel strong enough to apologize and be accountable. This dynamic can be especially intense between teen girls and moms, whom you love and need but who also seem to trigger your annoyance.

This is where the beautiful and soothing Hawaiian ritual called the Ho'oponopono comes in. It's a four-line Hawaiian prayer that soothes you and brings you back into alignment with your core self—the *you* beyond the stress and irritability that are so normal and understandable. Repeating the four lines has a soothing effect that ripples back to the people you love.

Give it a try now. Some teens like to put on quiet music to set the mood. Because this ritual is borrowed from Hawaiian culture, Hawaiian music works well. Bring to mind someone you've been annoyed and impatient with. Repeat these four lines either silently out loud while thinking of them.

> I'm sorry.
>
> Please forgive me.
>
> I love you.
>
> Thank you.

Repeat as many times as it takes to feel a shift internally.

What person came to mind?

What about your relationship with this person feels stressful to you?

What did you notice after repeating the Ho'oponopono?

Now, try the practice again this time only with and toward yourself. Yes, yourself. All things flow from the relationship you have with yourself, and keeping it healthy and clear is extremely important to your mental health.

Give it a try and don't hold back.

> *I'm sorry.*
>
> *Please forgive me.*
>
> *I love you.*
>
> *Thank you.*

How did it feel to focus the four lines on yourself? Did you notice any shifts in your body, your thoughts, or your feelings?

NOTE OF ENCOURAGEMENT:

Mental health isn't the absence of uncomfortable feelings. Mental health is the ability to feel your feelings, honor them, and allow them to move through you *without getting stuck and without allowing them to drive you into unhealthy habits and behaviors*. Next time you get stuck in anger toward yourself or others, explore the power of soothing your soul with a heartfelt apology. It's as simple as this: *I'm sorry. You didn't deserve that.*

CHAPTER 3

Upgrade Your Morning Routine

66

Well begun is half done.

—Aristotle

99

66

If I have a bad morning, the
rest of my day is shit.

—Emme, age seventeen

99

 **LEARN**

Very few teenagers claim to be "morning people," but did you know there is a biological reason why mornings may be hell for you? Unlike adults and younger kids, your teen brain releases the sleepy chemical melatonin up to ninety minutes later at night. So, if you're up way past your parents' bedtime these days, that's less weird than you think. At the same time, getting less than eight to ten hours of sleep leaves you vulnerable to more than just sleepiness in class. Your emotions will feel more intense and harder to manage. Your personality will feel flat and uninspired, and your ability to feel your best will be limited.

You just can't enjoy good mental health when your mind and body don't get enough time to rest and reset. Feeling tired and feeling depressed have a *lot* in common.

If getting enough sleep is a challenge for you, instead of waking up to a comforting routine to start your day, you wake up late, stressed, and already behind. Some teens feel a sense of morning dread that is overwhelming and literally nauseating. What a perfect time for your next mental health habit. With a little planning and attention, you can swap panic for peace, so your mornings are your soft start to a much better day.

 **REFLECT**

Do you take a proactive or reactive approach to your morning routine? *Proactive* means you have a plan that you follow. *Reactive* means you don't really have a plan, or if you do have a plan, it's not strictly followed. Proactive mode feels calm and organized. You may not feel awake and ready to seize the day, but you're following your plan with relative sanity. Reactive mode feels chaotic and crisis oriented. There might be a loose plan in there somewhere, but it's hit or miss, with emphasis on *miss*.

Place a heart to represent where you are on the scale below:

Stressed and   I have a routine but have a   I have a
chaotic.   hard time sticking to it.   strong routine.

If you're more proactive/reactive/mixed, do you see that approach in other areas of your life? Where? (This could be schoolwork, keeping your space organized, managing commitments.)

_____

_____

_____

How does a proactive/reactive approach feel when you're in it? How is it working or not working for you?

_____

_____

_____

_____

EXPLORE

Let's take this further...

Imagine a calm and efficient school-day morning. Imagine yourself easily moving through all the various things you do to set yourself up for a good day. Describe what you envision:

_____

_____

_____

_____

What are the factors, both inside and outside your control, that set you up for this wonderful morning?

Recall the most recent hell morning you've had—what went wrong?

How did your hell morning affect you? How did it affect the rest of your day? Did you shake it off and reset, or did you remain rattled? Get into detail here:

Many teens are chronically exhausted from too much homework or screen time and not enough sleep. Reflecting on yourself, what do you observe?

Sleep is widely believed to have a huge impact on mental health for people of all ages, *but especially teenagers.* What do you observe?

On a scale of 1 to 10, rate how much sleep affects you in the following areas (1 means "not at all" and 10 means "very strongly"):

_____ **PHYSICALLY**   _____ **SOCIALLY**   _____ **ACADEMICALLY**

_____ **YOUR MOOD**   _____ **YOUR PERSONALITY**   _____ **YOUR PATIENCE**

If you intentionally created a kinder, more efficient and effective morning for yourself, what would the biggest upside be?

NOTE OF ENCOURAGEMENT: Routines are helpful because they protect you from *decision fatigue,* a decreased ability to make good decisions over the course of a day. When you set up a morning routine that you really like, you protect yourself from needing to make a bunch of tiny little choices and decisions so early in the day. As you know, morning decisions are often *not the best* when every cell in your body is urging you to stay in bed as long as possible.

ELEVATE

To set yourself up for a day of feeling your best, design your ideal morning routine by choosing from the following morning routine menu.

• • • Morning Routine Menu • • •

FRESHEN UP OPTIONS TO RAMP UP YOUR ENERGY:

- Wash your face
- Take a shower
- Finish your shower with cold water (This boosts the feel-good chemical dopamine and helps mood and focus!)

HYDRATION:

Did you know that most people are chronically dehydrated and that you're most dehydrated when you wake up? Hydration ideas to support your mood, memory, and metabolism:

- Warm or hot water with lemon
- Herbal tea
- Miso soup (grab some miso paste from the store, so all you need to add is some hot water. This is great for when you wake up without an appetite or feeling nauseous. Mix it in a travel mug and sip it throughout the morning!)
- Bone broth (good for focus and energy)

HONOR YOUR BODY WITH BREAKFAST:

- Oatmeal, overnight oats
- Eggs
- Toast with avocado or nut butter

What breakfast options work for you? (No skipping allowed!)

BONUS TIME!

When you get right up and stay on track, you may find you have a few minutes for you time. Ideas for this time include pleasure reading, a short meditation, stretching or gentle exercise, reviewing the day ahead, organizing your backpack, prepping a snack, listening to music, time with a pet.

My Ideal Routine

Choose from the menu or create your own!

WAKE-UP TIME _____

 MY PLAN TO FRESHEN UP:

 MY PLAN FOR HYDRATION:

 MY PLAN FOR BREAKFAST:

 MY BONUS MORNING TIME!

Is there anything you can do the night before that will make your morning easier? To set yourself up for max success, list what you can do the night before:

1.

2.

3.

4.

5.

6.

7.

Now that's proactive!

 ## Challenge: ELIMINATE MORNING MEDIA

Waking up and checking social media is a common go-to for many teens. Don't worry, this challenge is not suggesting that you eliminate social media from your life altogether— although your mental health would *love it*. This challenge is merely suggesting you eliminate it from *your morning*. Why? There is something about waking up to social media (or excessive time on your phone) that throws off your whole day. Teen girls often share that scrolling not only makes them late but increases anxiety and lowers their mood for the rest of the day.

Your days are challenging enough. Why start them with stress you can easily avoid? Well, maybe not *easily*. It's a big move on your part, with a tremendous mental health upside. Teen girls immediately notice that saving social media until later has a huge impact on their ability to follow their morning routine in peace *and* on how they feel the rest of the day. Do you accept this challenge?

I ACCEPT!

If you're not on social media, are there any other time-sucks you'd like to eliminate as your challenge?

TIME-SUCKS:

◎ _____

◎ _____

◎ _____

◎ _____

Any emotional reaction(s) to this challenge? 😊 😐 🙁 ☹️ 😣

_____

_____

_____

_____

_____

Do you often/rarely allow feelings of resistance to stop you from doing things you know are good for you? Give a few examples.

Give an example of when you felt resistance but chose the best action or behavior anyway. Include how it felt and what the result was.

QUESTIONS TO PONDER: Are you willing to explore making stronger decisions on your own behalf to improve your life? In other words, hold yourself accountable instead of flaking on what's best for you? Can you experience resistance without "obeying" it? Notice how you feel in your body as you ponder these questions.

What feelings are you noticing right now? Are you feeling challenged? Is that okay with you?

Remember the affirmation *I can do hard things*? You can do hard things, and you can hold yourself accountable without flaking. Sometimes you need to suffer in the little picture so you can *thrive* in the big one!

Write about the results of this challenge below:

 ## PSYCH TIP: REVERSE ENGINEER YOUR EVENING

Unlike when you were a little girl and could fall asleep in an amusement park, you may have a harder time turning your brain off these days. Many girls share that their brain turns into a squirrel show of thoughts and worries, preventing the thing they need the most—*sleep*!

Here's where your psych tip comes in. Reverse engineering your evening means starting with the end in mind (sleep) and working backwards.

START WITH THE END GOAL

To determine your lights-out time, count backwards nine hours from your wake-up time. Yes, nine hours is recommended for your age. Nine hours helps your memory work best for school *and* it helps your emotions behave themselves.

FOR EXAMPLE:

7:00 a.m.	-	(9 hrs.)	=	10:00 p.m.
My wake-up time	*-*	*my sleep goal*	*=*	*lights-out*

POWER OFF DEVICES (POD)

To calm the squirrel, devices need to get powered off one hour before lights-out. Otherwise, you're asking your squirrel to nap at a circus. Set yourself up for a successful night of restorative sleep by powering down. Yes, this takes major discipline. Yes, it is worth it! You'll end up feeling *so much better*, and few girls feel that they're missing anything of true value.

FOR EXAMPLE:

10:00 p.m.	-	(1 hr.)	=	9:00 p.m.
My lights-out	*-*	*1 hour*	*=*	*POD*

CALMING TECH-FREE ACTIVITIES

At first, you may feel unexcited by screen-free activities, and that's to be expected. Devices are popular for a reason. Be strong because no one *ever* regrets this upgrade to their evening routine. When you get over the hump of initial despair, you'll grow to *love* your tech-free calming activities. This part of your routine is *you* time that calms your squirrel while replenishing your body and soul.

There are so many things you can do between POD and lights-out. A few examples include art or coloring, knitting, crafting, reading for pleasure, meditating, writing in a journal, soaking in a bath. If you're not sure what to choose, consider a book you can read for pleasure. Have fun asking people about books, and find a series to fall in love with. Reading is a wonderful way to engage your mind while relaxing your nervous system.

What are some screen-free activities you can put into your evening routine?

TEETH AND SKIN (YOUR NIGHTLIES)

Many girls report great success in going straight to the bathroom for their "nightlies" *immediately after* powering off devices. Switching gears purposefully to focus on new tasks is a brain hack that helps you redirect any feelings of withdrawal that come with shutting down devices. Your nightlies include whatever you do (teeth, skin care, bath or shower) before going to bed. Some girls just check this off their list quickly, and other girls enjoy a more elaborate routine. What does your routine include?

Do you like your routine as is, or do you want to add or subtract anything?

NOTE OF ENCOURAGEMENT:
Sticking to a new routine can feel unnatural at first. Some teens feel like they're going through withdrawal when they make healthy boundaries with their devices to elevate their sleep and overall mental health. It helps if you expect a certain amount of discomfort and then stick to your new routine. Trust that making the best decisions for yourself will feel more natural over time.

How much time do your nightlies require?

Next up: Test your knowledge on something you do all day, every day, and even in your sleep.

?

POP QUIZ: THINKING FACTS

While protecting your sleep helps you think better, it doesn't necessarily help you think *less*. You know better than anyone how much thinking you do all day, every day, and while some thinking is obviously good and necessary, there's lots and lots of thinking that's useless and painful.

Circle each of the following statements as T for true or F for false:

1. T / F As a teenager, you have up to five thousand thoughts a day.

2. T / F It's important to pay attention to your thoughts because they offer you accurate information on which to base your feelings and actions.

3. T / F The only difference between a "regular" thought and an "obsessive" thought is how much attention you give it.

4. T / F Falling in love and "crushing" creates a lot of overthinking, which is normal.

5. T / F Your patterns of thinking have a lot to do with how you feel about yourself, other people, and life.

Answers:

1. **False**: You likely have closer to *seventy thousand* thoughts a day!

2. **False**: While it's true that thoughts ignite feelings, many thoughts are complete garbage, especially if you fall into common teen thinking traps (more on those later). Yes, you need to think in order to navigate life. No, you don't need to believe everything you think, because a lot of your thoughts are absolutely unhelpful and inaccurate, *especially* when you're stressed and emotional.

3. **True**: If you are a worrier, this is good news. You can remind yourself that just because your mind is obsessing on a thought, that doesn't make it true. When you give this thought less attention by redirecting your mind in healthier ways, it will fade just like regular thoughts.

4. **True**: Big crushes and falling in love can take over your thoughts, which, while intoxicating, can also make it hard to feel balanced.

5. **True**: Teens are often shocked to discover how much of their emotional pain comes not from reality but from their thoughts about reality. Instead of believing everything you think, begin to ask yourself, *Wait, is this thought even true?*

NOTE OF ENCOURAGEMENT: The takeaway here is that while many thoughts are useful and accurate, many are not. Believing everything you think is not wise. When you have an upsetting thought, slow down and take an objective look at it. Remind yourself that just because you think it, that doesn't make it true. Try writing down upsetting thoughts to get them out of your head. Then, reallocate your attention in a healthier direction.

CHAPTER 4

Check Self-Limiting Beliefs

> 66
>
> If you accept a limiting belief,
> it will become a truth for you.
>
> —Louise Hay
>
> 99

> 66
>
> I always thought that my brother
> was smart and I wasn't, so I
> didn't even try in school.
>
> —Leah, age fifteen
>
> 99

 **LEARN**

As you know, you have approximately seventy thousand thoughts a day. Some are accurate, true, and supportive of your mental health. *Many* are inaccurate, untrue, and unhelpful to your mental health. Thoughts that are on auto-repeat in your head often become ⟶ *beliefs*. For example, if you think of yourself as "not smart" enough times, that thought becomes a belief that influences the decisions you make and the actions you take. Like fifteen-year-old Leah, you might not try in school.

Similarly, if you have the thought often enough that you're socially awkward, you will begin to believe it—and that belief will influence the decisions you make and the actions you take (or don't take), which then create your reality.

Whew! That is a powerful chain to examine, because there is so much room for error in your thoughts, and if you don't catch the error (aka *thinking trap*), your life will be shaped by beliefs that come from thoughts that are inaccurate, untrue, or unsupportive of your mental health!

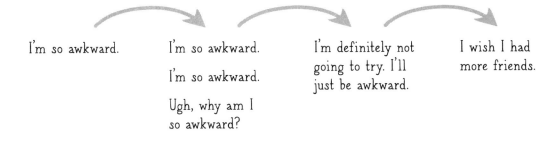

I'm so awkward.

I'm so awkward.

I'm so awkward.

Ugh, why am I so awkward?

I'm definitely not going to try. I'll just be awkward.

I wish I had more friends.

If this makes you think more deeply about the reality you're creating, that's good, because your life doesn't need to be limited by beliefs that work against you. When you begin a habit of catching and elevating negative thoughts, you prevent them from becoming self-limiting beliefs. What about thoughts that have *already become* self-limiting beliefs? You can begin a habit of challenging them and changing them into something more accurate and supportive.

 **REFLECT**

Reflect on thoughts/beliefs you have about yourself that hold you back. Fill in the blanks below:

I tend to think that I'll feel better about myself if I _____

_____

Because in the past I experienced _____ ,

now I struggle to feel confident about _____

One of the repetitive negative thoughts I have about myself is _____

_____

Choose one of the three statements that you just completed, and write about it in more detail, including any thoughts, feelings, insights, or examples that come up for you.

_____

_____

_____

_____

_____

_____

Good work building self-reflection skills. Now you're going to dive deeper into three types of self-limiting beliefs that were touched upon here.

 **EXPLORE**

THE IF/WHEN MISTAKE

If you're holding yourself back from something because you've decided (or somebody told you) that you need to be "different" before going for what you want, you may be suffering from an *if/when* belief. Explore this possibility by finishing the sentences below.

What "boxes" do you believe need to be checked for you to feel good about yourself?

☐ *I'd feel good about myself academically if I:*

_____

☐ *I'd feel confident about myself socially if I:*

_____

☐ *I'd be content with my appearance if I:*

_____

☐ *I'd feel better about myself as a person if I:*

_____

Any other boxes you feel need to be checked before you feel good about yourself?

☐ _____

☐ _____

☐ _____

☐ _____

Do you suspect you stay trapped in one or more of these self-limiting beliefs because trapped is more comfortable than putting yourself out there and making braver choices? Explore what's true for you, and write about it.

Unchallenged, the thoughts or beliefs you've identified keep you stuck in a low mood, low self-confidence, low healthy risk-taking, and high anxiety. Challenging thoughts and beliefs with questions can help you see more of the truth. Explore what challenging a self-limiting belief feels like by taking one of your if/then thoughts and writing it here:

Now, answer these questions to challenge your self-limiting belief:

Is this box truly as important as I make it out to be?

Am I sure this box isn't checked or partially checked already? What's the evidence that it's checked or partially checked already?

Who do I know who doesn't have this box checked, but I don't judge them? Who do I know who hasn't checked this box, yet they move forward and go for what they want anyway?

Is it even true that I have to check this box before I feel better, feel braver, or make more powerful choices? Can I just feel better, be braver, or make more powerful choices now? *And then I can work on checking the box or accepting that the box doesn't need to be checked?*

If I move forward without waiting for this box to be checked, what would I do that's different (braver) than what I do now? What actions or choices would I make?

What might braver action bring me that I'd like to have happen? Get into detail here.

THE THEN = NOW MISTAKE

Now for the next common mistake that causes teen girls to limit themselves. Are there experiences from your past that have caused you to hold negative thoughts and self-limiting beliefs about yourself? You may need to really think about this. Circle one: Yes   No

Describe this experience or these experiences. How old were you? What happened?

_____

_____

_____

_____

How did this experience or these experiences influence the way you think of yourself, your value, or what you're capable of?

_____

_____

_____

_____

What would happen if you decided to honor these experiences, hold them with love and appreciation for what you went through, and move forward anyway?

_____

_____

_____

_____

What happens if you stay where you are? What is the win for you? The loss for you?

What would that look like six months from now?

A year from now?

♥

NOTE OF ENCOURAGEMENT: Your mental health improves when you open your heart to what you've been through, let go of any self-limiting beliefs that came from those experiences, and intentionally create more encouraging beliefs, such as That was hard, but I got through it! Try it out and see how it feels.

It was hard, but I got through it!

THE NEGATIVITY TRAP

Do you hold negative thoughts that are inaccurate, unhelpful, or just plain false? It's time to upgrade those thoughts to something more accurate, helpful, and supportive to your mental health! Check out the examples below and give it a try with your own negative thoughts.

WRITE YOUR NEGATIVE THOUGHT.

WRITE A MORE REALISTIC AND SUPPORTIVE UPGRADE FOR THAT THOUGHT.

I'm so awkward, I want to go home.

➡️ It's okay to feel awkward. I'll warm up and feel more comfy.

I don't want to raise my hand in class, because I don't want people to judge me.

➡️ What other people think of me is their business. I'll focus on myself and what I want to say.

I'm not as smart/pretty/fit as they are, so it's hard to be around them.

➡️ I will "stay in my lane" and not get sucked into comparing myself. We all have our own value.

➡️

➡️

➡️

NOTE OF ENCOURAGEMENT: Noticing negative thoughts and upgrading them is one of your most powerful mental health habits.

 **ELEVATE**

Are there any *new actions* you can take to support your upgraded thoughts? For example, when Leah realized her thinking was limiting her, she began putting more effort into school. Her growth from then on was enormous. Leah found that while she is not the math genius her brother is, she loves to write and has been making huge improvements in her writing skills. As a bonus, expressing herself through writing has helped her feel more confident and able to express herself in relationships. This is a great example of how one good thing leads to another.

Is there a new action or behavior you'd like to energize in your life? One that supports the thoughts you're elevating?

What's the biggest challenge in following through with the new action or behavior?

How will you overcome it?

Imagine a *future you* being interviewed about what's changed since committing to the new action or behavior. What does your future self say about the change and the impact it's made?

Draw a stick figure picture of you in the new action/behavior. Draw anything that comes to you. Keep it quick and lighthearted, because drawing is a way to involve your creative brain, and this is for self-expression, not artistic evaluation.

Good for you! You've brought thought and energy in contemplating your growth. Are you committed?

Challenge: STICK TO NEW HABITS

To convert a behavior to a habit, it helps to create reminders that support the repetition of the behavior. Repetition is everything.

Write three upgraded beliefs on sticky notes or index cards and sprinkle them liberally around your personal spaces. You can sneak them onto a corner of a school notebook or on your phone, as a reminder, and in private places like your underwear drawer. New thoughts need attention, so they can develop into beliefs, so sprinkle away!

Choose your upgraded beliefs:

_____

_____

_____

Where you will put them?

_____

_____

_____

Feel free to switch out your notes for new ones, so you can keep this mental health habit fresh and fun. When it comes to guiding your mind in the right direction, it's all about practice and repetition.

Now for your next mental health challenge...

PSYCH TIP: FOCUS SWITCHING

Have you ever had an episode of awkwardness or self-consciousness that felt so intense, you felt panicky inside? These painful flare-ups are an excruciatingly common part of teen development that thankfully fade as your brain matures. They're triggered by anything from a jokey comment (at your expense) to seeing yourself in a picture and hating the way you look. Rationally, you tell yourself to let it go and move on, but your anxiety just doesn't seem to get the message. To shift out of these painful flare-ups of self-focus, this tip is a life saver.

Give it a try now so you understand how it works:

STEP 1: For about ten seconds, close your eyes, plug your ears, and notice everything happening *inside your body*. The speed and intensity of your heartbeat, details about your breathing, your body tension, any noticeable observations about your digestion—you get the idea. Get granular with your observations because the point is to notice as much as possible. When you've concluded your ten seconds of intense inner focus, open your eyes and list everything you can about what you noticed.

STEP 2:
Good job! Now, for
about ten seconds and with your eyes
open, focus on everything you can outside
yourself. Name as many
objects as you can by
their color or other
characteristic, for
example: *white
bookshelf, blue bedspread,
cute cat, beige wall, flower
pillow, brown desk, tall glass.*
After ten seconds, fill the spaces
with everything you observed.

When you switched your attention from inside yourself to outside yourself, what did you notice about your connection to your body sensations?

_____

_____

_____

_____

_____

_____

When you're feeling okay, focusing inside yourself feels neutral, but when you're feeling self-conscious or socially anxious, teen girls share that it's hell. It's like being trapped in a distorted version of yourself where all your flaws and vulnerabilities are greatly exaggerated. In such moments, it's easy to get convinced that there's really a problem—when the "problem" is actually creating itself because your focus is trapped. But now you have an escape hatch...

Next flare-up, instead of being held hostage, firmly *take control of your focus* and shift into your external environment. This is called *attention shifting*, and practicing it as a new habit will make you a pro.

NOTE OF ENCOURAGEMENT: Practice attention switching whenever you can. When you're scrolling on your phone and someone comes in the room or speaks to you, switch your attention from your phone to the person. When you're feeling stuck in bed, and you need to get up, practice switching your focus to *getting up and only getting up*. When you find yourself obsessing about what could go wrong, switch your focus to what could go right! Focus is like a muscle that gets stronger the more you "work out," so practice and it will be ready when you need it!

～ SOUL SOOTHER: TENSE AND RELAX

Ever notice that when you feel a wave of stress, or a jolt of anxiety, the muscles in your body automatically tense up? That tensing is a sign that your brain is perceiving stress as danger, so it's ramping up your body in preparation to fight or run for your life. This *fight-or-flight* response is natural, but it doesn't help when you're feeling stressed, because tensing up leads to symptoms like headaches, muscle soreness, and fatigue.

The goal of this soul soother is for you to get better at distinguishing a tense state from a relaxed state, so you can intentionally shift into a relaxed state whenever you want. The benefit is two-fold: (1) Your physical body will feel better, and (2) Your stress and anxiety will decrease because your calm body will send messages to your brain that you're actually safe. You may be stressed, but you're safe.

Give it a try. Do this exercise when you have at least ten minutes to focus on yourself without being interrupted. Pick a chair, couch, or bed where you can completely relax.

Starting with your feet, curl your toes downward and contract the muscles of your feet while inhaling through your nose (if you can) for a count of five. Then release those the muscles in your feet while exhaling (through your mouth) for another count of five. Got it?

NOTE OF ENCOURAGEMENT: The best part of the tense and relax is that you are now in charge of cueing a greater state of calm whenever you need it. If you want to go through all the muscle groups, go for it. You can also just focus on the muscle group or groups that are most relevant to you—or the ones you can clench and relax before a test without anyone else noticing. Don't wait until you're stressed and anxious. Practice this soul soother at least once a day, so it's an easy go-to when you need it! When it comes to your access to feeling better in hard moments, you are as powerful as your strategies and habits, and you've got quite a list going. Add this one to your list.

Now let's hit all the major muscle groups. Repeat the five-second inhale as you focus on:

- **LOWER LEGS AND FEET:** Tighten calf muscles by pulling toes toward you. Five-second exhale and relax.

- **UPPER LEGS:** Squeeze thigh muscles. Five-second exhale and relax.

- **HANDS:** Clench your fists. Five-second exhale and relax.

- **ARMS:** Tighten your biceps by drawing your forearms up toward your shoulders while clenching fists. Five-second exhale and relax.

- **BUTT MUSCLES:** Tighten your butt muscles. Five-second exhale and relax.

- **STOMACH:** Tense your stomach muscles (as if anticipating a punch). Five-second exhale and relax.

- **CHEST:** Take a deep breath to tighten. Five-second exhale and relax.

- **NECK AND SHOULDERS:** Raise your shoulders up toward your ears. Five-second exhale and relax.

- **MOUTH:** Open your mouth wide enough to stretch the hinges of your jaw. Five-second exhale and relax.

- **EYES:** Clench your eyelids tightly shut. Five-second exhale and relax.

- **FOREHEAD:** Raise your eyebrows as far upward as you can. Five-second exhale and relax.

★ MOOD TIPS FROM TEENS ★

Madi, age seventeen: *"I used to be totally powerless over my mood, but I've really changed that over the past year. I just got tired of feeling so helpless, so I tried a bunch of things. Here is my favorite: Focus on someone around me and even though it's hard, shift my attention to that person. This is my number one because it gets me out of my own head and I find that being a good friend to someone else lifts my mood."*

CHAPTER 5

Build
Self-Confidence

"

We see the world, not as
it is, but as we are.

—Stephen R. Covey

"

My self-confidence is based on
liking myself and not on my
achievements. But I've had
to work at that.

—Haley, age nineteen

"

 **LEARN**

If you'd like more self-confidence, you're not alone. Moving from childhood to the teen years is a time when many girls experience a sharp (and painful) plunge of self-confidence. Instead of feeling open to new people and opportunities, you may pull back—to protect yourself from feeling uncomfortable, judged, or self-conscious. Instead of feeling fine being you, you may experience more self-doubt and insecurity than you did when you were younger. Life gets more complicated when girls move from childhood to the teen years, and though boys have their challenges too, our current culture presents more stressors for girls. It's not surprising self-confidence takes a hit.

REFLECT

Reflecting on your self-confidence, have you noticed a change? If so, when did that begin? What do you remember about that time?

Many girls have specific memories of incidents where they were bullied or criticized, and while most people think it's girls who are mean to each other, a lot of bullying toward girls comes from boys! Do you have any specific memories that come to mind? This might feel emotionally loaded for you so remind yourself that you are safe in this moment. Imagine you are moving any pain you're feeling from inside you to outside you, through the journaling process.

If your self-confidence didn't take a hit, or if it improved, that happens sometimes! Write about how this unfolded for you. Were there factors that supported your confidence in blossoming?

Decrease
in healthy risk-taking
(trying new things/meeting
new people/speaking in class) ____

EXPLORE

When teen girls lack
confidence, they
often sprout new
ways to cope with
their higher levels of
self-consciousness
and insecurity.
Unfortunately, some
of these attempts to
cope become lifelong
habits that negatively
affect confidence
and mental health.

Are you coping
in ways that don't
support your
confidence and
mental health?

Check out these
different habits and
rate each on a scale
of 1 to 10, with 1
signifying it's not a
coping habit for you
and 10 signifying it's a
coping habit
you use often. Fill
the rest of each space
with any thoughts,
feelings, or examples
that come to mind.

Increase
in perfectionism ____

Increase
in overthinking ____

Increase
in procrastination ____

Increase
in people-pleasing ____

Decrease
in accepting
compliments ____

 **ELEVATE**

The good news about confidence is that you can build it by trading unhelpful habits for better ones. Explore each confidence-boosting habit below and share your thoughts.

LEAVE YOUR COMFORT ZONE

If you're a little too attached to your comfort zone, sticking only with the people and activities that you know, this is understandable, but it's not growth oriented. You can't grow if you're avoiding opportunities for growth, and as you've probably heard, the only true failure is in not trying.

To grow your self-confidence, it's time to extend yourself in ways that aren't quite comfortable. That means saying YES instead of "No way," for example, to some of the activities listed on the right.

Which of the above most speaks to you?

- Trying out for a team/a play/other activity
- Joining a club
- Starting a conversation with someone new ("Hi" counts)
- Applying for a part-time job or volunteer work
- Speaking up in class
- Complimenting someone with warmth and sincerity
- Initiating conversations with people you know or would like to know better, showing interest in them
- Being more of your true self instead of who others expect you to be
- Letting people know you better by being more open
- Going for what you want

Using the above examples for inspiration, what are a few ways you want to stretch out of your comfort zone?

How would this help you grow? How would it benefit you?

Are there stretches you've already made? Give yourself credit and name as many as you can think of, even if they don't sound that impressive to you.

How did doing these things affect your feelings about yourself and what you're capable of?

NOTE OF ENCOURAGEMENT: It's natural to feel anxious or scared when you're growing. Remember that you'll often experience fear *with no actual danger or threat to your safety.* As you stretch outside your comfort zone, you'll encounter the *perceived danger* of uncomfortable feelings, which you can handle! Real danger, on the other hand, is something to avoid. Getting out of your comfort zone need not involve risky or reckless behavior. Take good care of yourself.

REFRAME FAILURE

Reframing is a strategy that involves changing your thoughts about something, so you can see it in a new, more open-minded, and productive way. Reframing failure looks something like:

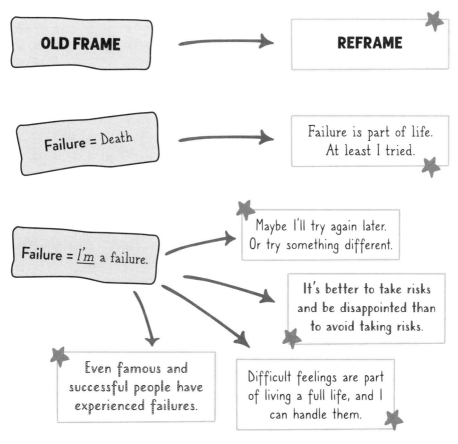

Instead of (or in addition to) fearing failure, many girls fear the following. How about you? Circle all that apply:

being judged	looking stupid	feeling self-conscious	feeling scared	making a mistake
feeling exposed	feeling visible	getting rejected	feeling vulnerable	falling short

Say more about what you circled. Any thoughts, feelings, or memories that come up for you?

_____

_____

_____

_____

_____

_____

_____

_____

_____

_____

_____

Are you ready to reframe failure? First take a look at this real-life example.

ARI'S OLD FRAME: Ari, age sixteen, wanted to run for student council but convinced herself that she not only would look stupid if she ran but also would probably lose and die of disappointment and shame.

ARI'S REFRAME: "My older brother was on student council, but he was also very popular and outgoing. I want to run for an office, but there's a chance that not enough people know me well enough to vote for me. If I run but don't make it, I'll be disappointed but probably also proud that I tried. I can also run again next year and have a better chance because I'll know more people. I can use the time in between to work on getting to know more people."

Your turn. Start by identifying something you'd like to explore, do, or be that you're holding yourself back from. Include whatever self-limiting thoughts or beliefs you notice.

Now write a reframe (as Ari did) that is more encouraging and supportive of you. Hint: you can accept the fear and potential disappointment and carry on with life.

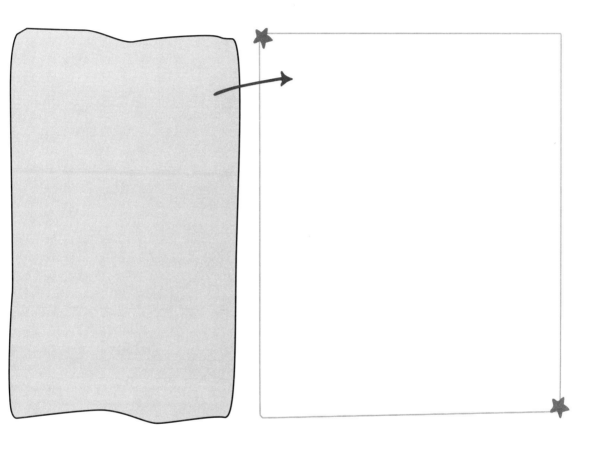

NOTE OF ENCOURAGEMENT: You'll feel better when your perspective is more flexible, open, and creative. Once you get good at reframing, you'll be able to extend your ability to think flexibly to people in your life. For example, your friend is devastated over a big disappointment. You validate their feelings and then offer to point out another possibility. With their consent, you offer a reframe. This is a great example of how, in building good mental health habits, you can help others too.

PULL BACK PEOPLE-PLEASING

People-pleasing is the habit of trying (too hard) to make others happy. In contrast to authentic kindness, going *too far* to please others is often fear driven. People-pleasers often lose touch with their own needs because they're so focused on gaining a sense of their value through pleasing others.

Is people-pleasing a habit for you? Give yourself a 1 to 10 rating and write about your thoughts and feelings regarding how this habit affects you.

1 2 3 4 5 6 7 8 9 10

Who do you people-please the most, and why? And the least, and why?

What do you see as your motivations for people-pleasing?

What's your biggest fear if you pull back on people-pleasing? (Don't look for anything rational. Just trust what comes to you.)

Now, thinking realistically, how likely is that fear? Place an X where you fall on the scale below:

Unlikely   Likely

NOTE OF ENCOURAGEMENT: If anxiety arises as you pull back on people-pleasing, it's because your nervous system is registering a *perceived danger* that you'll be negatively affected if you fail to please. This part of the human brain is very primitive, so it's kind of dramatic about sensing danger. Your job is to use the logical part of your brain to soothe the fear and put it into perspective. For example: *I'm stronger than I think, and even if that happened, I could get through it.* BTW, it's more likely that the opposite will happen: people will value you *more* because excessive people-pleasing is a sign of low self-confidence and low self-worth. When you don't value yourself, unfortunately, others often follow your lead.

TAKE IN THE POSITIVE

When you're feeling bad, it's easy to get stuck because of something called a *negativity bias*. It means your brain notices and amplifies everything negative while missing or dismissing the stuff that would feel good if you let it in.

How are you at taking compliments? How do you respond to a compliment?

How are you at giving compliments? Who do you compliment and what kind of compliments do you give?

When you give someone a heartfelt compliment, how do you like them to respond?

Think of something specific you can commit to saying next time you receive a compliment. A sentence to hold in your pocket that's ready to go:

⭐ **EXTRA CREDIT:** Take in an acknowledgment or a compliment fully and completely: not just with your ears but with an open heart to the giver and yourself as the receiver. Accept it as the gift that it is and allow it to nourish you. If you're uncomfortable, that's okay! It just means you need to grow in this area. Like all habits, accepting compliments gets easier with practice. Okay, one more question...

How are you at acknowledging yourself? Take a moment to feel good about yourself for who you are or what you've done:

If you got better at healthy, loving self-acknowledgment, how might it benefit you?

Many teen girls believe that their achievements are worthy of acknowledgment, and that's it. If you relate, consider opening your heart to the many sweet, funny, clever, kind, and creative aspects of yourself that transcend achievement. Achievements are great, but they're what you do, not *who you are*. Every now and then, catch yourself in a small moment of being uniquely you. Acknowledge and appreciate yourself.

For example, acknowledge yourself for: An act of thoughtfulness. An act of kindness. A moment of extreme patience. Making someone laugh. Laughing at yourself. A heartfelt apology. An act of bravery. For taking responsibility instead of being defensive. For cleaning up something you don't feel like cleaning up. For doing something in a way that only you do it. For any and all of your lovable quirks.

NOTE OF ENCOURAGEMENT: Letting good stuff in is food for self-confidence. Here are some other nutrients for self-confidence: hanging out with positive, kind, supportive people; spending time in nature to clear your mind and connect with yourself; practicing patience and kindness toward yourself; improving your posture as you walk through your life; making eye contact with people and learning to hold it; using your voice to speak up or make boundaries. Working on these things positively affects your mood, your relationships, and your self-confidence. Building confidence is a lifelong pursuit that you are starting NOW. Take a nice inhale and breathe in acknowledgment for the work you're doing.

Challenge: ACTING AS IF

Acting as if is a form of "fake it till you make it" that helps you practice the growth-oriented, more confident version of yourself. Here's how it works.

Think of three areas of your life where you'd like to feel more confident:

1. _____

2. _____

3. _____

Choosing one of these three areas, explain how your confident self feels, speaks, looks, sounds, moves, and interacts. You can think of this version of you as your *preferred self*, the you that you are growing into. Think deeply and in detail, because your brain loves this movie you're making in your mind and is wiring for it. What are you imagining?

_____

_____

_____

Now that you have clarity about how your confidence looks and feels, your challenge is to act as if it were all true. With the new brain wiring your imagination has created, you have a strong head start!

Is *acting as if* the same as being fake? No, because *it becomes true as you create it.* Much of what has become reality started with your creative imagination, followed up with action. Put this challenge into action as soon as you can and come back to write about your experience or breakthrough.

What was your *acting as if* experience like?

Feel free to take this challenge to those other areas where you'd like to feel more confident. There's no stopping you now.

PSYCH TIP: IMPORT YOUR INSPIRATIONAL OTHER

This psych tip provides even more support for boosting your confidence and bravery. It's not only extremely effective but also easy to master in just three easy steps:

1. Think of something you want to do or try but lack the confidence for. For example, you'd like to talk to or flirt with someone you're interested in. You'd like to skillfully stand up to someone making homophobic comments. You'd like to confidently raise your hand in class. You'd like to say "No thanks" instead of "Sure," when no is your genuine answer.

2. Decide on your inspirational other (IO). Using the first example, a good IO is someone you consider to be an excellent flirt. Your IO could be a friend, an acquaintance, a famous person, a character from a show or a movie or even a book.

3. As you think about the qualities this person has, imagine "importing" that person or those qualities into *you*. Imagine you have and own those exact qualities. Now, *take action* without overthinking. In this example, feel your inner flirt ignited and have fun with it.

The genius behind this tip is that you *already have* all that you need to act on your desire. You're just activating those qualities by connecting to your inspirational other.

Try it out now. Think of a situation in your life where you want to be braver and more confident as practice.

Your situation of choice: _____

_____

Now choose your inspirational other: _____

What qualities does your inspirational other have that you'd like to embody?

What action(s) will you take? (Don't take yourself too seriously. It gets in the way of creativity and progress.)

Excellent! Now, imagine that your future self is confident about the behavior you just wrote about. Very confident. How is she feeling about herself?

Good job trying new things.

 ## SOUL SOOTHER:

PURGE AND CURATE YOUR FRIEND'S SOCIAL MEDIA

This soul soother is a little different, because instead of working directly on your nervous system to calm yourself, you'll be working on an emotional environment you may give little thought to: your online emotional environment. While social media is often a popular go-to whenever girls are bored, stressed, or in need of a little connection and entertainment, its effects on how you feel are rarely neutral. To get the most out of this soul soother, generously access your imagination and creativity.

Imagine you have a friend who is struggling with moodiness, low self-esteem, and anxiety. Because she's having a hard time, she "escapes" by spending a lot of time on social media—*a lot!* Miraculously, she has the exact same social media as you, and you've been chosen as her social media curator. Your social media curatorial fee is a million dollars, so you're extremely committed to the task at hand.

The task? To curate all your struggling friend's social media platforms. Specifically, to unfollow/unsubscribe or mute accounts whose content fails to support her best mental health. But you're not stopping there. Because mental health is very vulnerable to what people absorb through their ears and eyes, you will also add and follow content that supports her in feeling better!

If you think cat videos are good for your friend's mental health, research cute cat influencers and have her follow them. If you think motivational speakers are just what she needs, research the best ones and add those. Uplifting quotes? Meditations? Healthy snack recipes? Exercise challenges? Travel destinations? Nervous system hacks? Psych tips? Time management support? Research and explore the best content creators, and add them for your friend. Execute this task as if a million dollars depended on it!

As you explore your task, record the results here. For the purge list, note any account or content you want to remove. Under "cost," note why you think that account or content is not in the best interest of your friend's mental health. For the add list, note the accounts you think would be uplifting, informative, and supportive of her mental health. Under "benefit," note why you think that account or content will be good for her.

PURGE LIST

Account/Content: Cost:

- [ ]
- [ ]
- [ ]
- [ ]
- [ ]
- [ ]
- [ ]

ADD LIST

Account/Content: Benefit:

- [ ]
- [ ]
- [ ]
- [ ]
- [ ]
- [ ]
- [ ]

NOTE OF ENCOURAGEMENT: What you absorb has a massive impact on how you think, feel, and act. While most teen girls readily admit that social media negatively impacts their focus, their self-confidence, and their mood, many simultaneously feel a sense of hopelessness over their ability to stop or change their use of social media. At this point in your mental health journey, you know a lot about habits—habits that support mental health and habits that threaten mental health. Protect what you're working so hard on by curating your own social media as if *you* were worth a million dollars, because you are!

✹ MOOD TIPS FROM TEENS ✹

Dylann, age sixteen: *"I'm working on lifting myself out of bad moods, because honestly I think some part of me likes them. It's like being sad gives me an excuse not to care about anything or anyone, but that attitude has not been good for me. It feeds on itself and gets me really stuck. One day I made a special album on my phone of all the pics that made me smile, because I just forget about everything good when I'm sad. Or good times don't feel real—it's hard to explain. Anyway, now I scroll through my album when I feel the need for a bigger, happier perspective."*

CHAPTER 6

Care for
Your Feelings

"

When we numb the painful emotions,
we also numb the positive emotions.

—Brené Brown

"

My feelings are like the
weather for me. I feel like
I have no control.

—Sienna, age seventeen

"

 **LEARN**

Do you ever feel emotionally numb, disconnected, or just plain shut down? Or the opposite? Overwhelmed by your feelings, as if drowning in a flood of them? Both ends of this spectrum (and everything in between) is normal in your teen years. Not always comfortable, but normal.

The secret truth about feelings (aka emotions) is that they're a lot like wild, unparented little kids. They can be intense and demanding. They can be unpredictable and overwhelming. They can also surprise you by going from out-of-control to completely numb. They don't play by rules, and they want what they want.

It's *a lot*, until you deeply understand the secret truth: your little wildlings need you. They need your love and acceptance, your interest, understanding, and guidance. They don't like to be denied, ignored, judged, minimized, invalidated, or criticized. Your wild ones need someone who cares for them and pays attention. Someone who accepts them and comforts them, and *you* are the absolute best person to do that.

 **REFLECT**

As you reflect on your emotional life, what do you notice?

Place a heart on the scale closest to the statement that best represents you:

I tend to avoid my emotions or feel shut down.	Yes to everything; I am the whole spectrum.	I often feel overwhelmed by my emotions.

How is that for you? What's it like being where you are on this spectrum?

_____

_____

_____

_____

 EXPLORE

Another secret about feelings? When you notice them, name them, accept them, and connect to where you feel them in your body, *they calm down*. They just feel wild when neglected. As you learn to notice, name, accept, and connect with your feelings, they will feel more manageable.

Read the name of the feelings contained in the boxes on the next page, pausing as you move from box to box. As odd as it sounds, create a relationship with each feeling, one by one. Let it know you see it, feel it, and accept it. In doing so, you're acknowledging and creating space for the feeling, without judgment, fear, or the need to control.

Say each feeling's name out loud and close your eyes to make a connection to where that feeling lives in your body. Your heart, your belly, your throat? This is sometimes called *attending and befriending* your feelings.

NOTE OF ENCOURAGEMENT: This is big! You are showing your feelings that you can turn *toward* them—meet them, greet them, and get to know them. There are no "bad" feelings, just less comfortable ones. Each one is worthy of your attention and care. When they get that care, they relax so that you can move on to other things.

ANGER	SADNESS	FEAR

HURT	PRIDE	HAPPINESS

DISAPPOINTMENT	INSECURITY	SELF-CONSCIOUSNESS

SATISFACTION	CONTENTMENT	JEALOUSY

SELF-DOUBT	LOVE	EXCITEMENT

Returning to your boxes, add notes about anything you noticed in the attending and befriending process. For example, where does the feeling "live" in your body? Does it have a color or shape? Is there a heavy quality or a light quality? Does it tingle, flutter, expand or contract? Does it feel heavy, light, or something in between?

For example, Hazel describes anxiety as fluttering in her chest, light and shapeless. Bridget describes anxiety as a dark heavy pit in her belly that doesn't move. Each of these girls has learned to turn toward their unique experience of anxiety, which paradoxically has helped them become less scared of it.

If exploring feelings in this way feels like a stretch, that's completely natural and to be expected. Most of us are not raised or taught to make friends with our feelings. Stick with this practice, even if it feels strange, and over time you'll feel the benefits!

 **ELEVATE**

Ready to go to the next level? Processing feelings is a powerful mental health habit that deepens your relationship with yourself and your emotions. It also helps feelings resolve, so you can feel your best.

Choose a challenging feeling you struggle with and write it here:

If you were babysitting a five-year-old cutie pie who was struggling with this feeling, what would you say to her to soothe the feeling? What would your voice sound like? What attitude and energy would you bring to her?

How did that feel? Was it easy or hard? What personal qualities did you bring to the challenge of soothing this child?

When you think about it, doesn't it make sense that you would be just as kind and soothing to yourself? Can you imagine talking to your feelings in a similar way to help them calm?

Feelings come and go all day, so you'll have plenty of opportunities to practice what you're learning. Big feelings are often most obvious and noticeable, so they're a good place to get started. Just pause and notice them like waves that move through you. They know what to do on their own. You're just helping them along with these four steps:

1. Notice and name them: for example, anger, hurt, jealousy, self-doubt.

2. Accept the feeling: there are no "bad" ones, and they all make sense when you learn to listen to them.

3. Connect to where the feeling lives in your body. You may even explore whether the feeling has a shape or color. Does it feel heavy or light? Does the feeling have movement, or is there a stickiness about how it feels in your body?

4. Offer it care. Does it want just a moment of attention, a hug from a friend, a soul-soothing exercise?

NOTE OF ENCOURAGEMENT: There's no need to be perfectionistic about processing your feelings. If you start with noticing and naming a few each day, you will be moving in the right direction. When ready, you can add accepting, connecting to where the emotion is in your body, and soothing emotions with care and attention. Honor the pace that's right for you.

Challenge: EMOTIONAL CHECK-INS

In your day-to-day life, there are probably a lot of different things you need to take care of. No wonder your feelings are neglected! This is where emotional check-ins come in. Making time in your day to pause, slow down your body and mind, and check in with your feelings has many benefits. The first thing most people notice is that they feel overall calmer—and now you know why. Feelings calm when they receive your attention.

1. Take a few slow, deep breaths to calm your mind and body. Imagine shifting your attention from your outside world to your inside world.

2. Check in with your body to notice any sensations or feelings that want your attention. You may want to stretch your body to get a sense of the feelings inside.

3. Ask the question either silently or out loud: *How am I feeling in this moment?* Be patient and open to anything you notice.

4. If a feeling or feelings arise, name, accept, and explore anything and everything you can about the feelings. Reminder: color, weight, movement.

5. Ask your feelings if they need anything further from you. Maybe it's something you can respond to in the moment—like a stretch or a self-hug. Often, feelings are satisfied in simply getting your caring attention.

6. Open your eyes. You did it!

As you become better acquainted with your feelings, an interesting thing often happens. This is especially surprising if you tend to bottle up feelings and resist opening up to people. As you become more open and friendly toward all your feelings, they're easier to journal about and talk about. Opening up to others feels more natural too. Being able to say "I feel really anxious and off today" not only acknowledges the feeling but also creates a moment of authentic connection that improves closeness in relationships.

How/when/where can you make time for an emotional check-in? Reminder: You can *tether it* to a solo activity you already do!

- Your bath or shower
- A solo breakfast
- Walking the dog
- Riding in the car

You can also do an emotional check-in around other people. It's more distracting, but possible. Explore practicing an emotional check-in once a day for seven days, and see how it feels. Return to this page and share your experience!

What I notice after one week of emotional check-ins:

 PSYCH TIP: **VISUALIZATION FOR STICKY FEELINGS**

This is a teen favorite for when you feel stuck in a feeling that just won't budge, even though you've done your best with the processing steps you've learned.

Visualization is a psychological technique that involves closing your eyes to create mental images designed to support you in various ways. Olympic athletes use visualization to enhance performance; golfers use it to improve their game. Now you can use it to work with a feeling that is demanding a lot of attention from you—only you'll get in charge of the feeling, instead of the other way around.

Read through all these steps before closing your eyes and exploring them through visualization:

1. With eyes closed, get a sense of where the feeling is in your body. Draw an imaginary circle around the feeling, so the energy of the feeling is inside the bubble.

2. Breathe in and out slowly. With every inhale, visualize (and feel) your feeling bubble expand. With every exhale, visualize (and feel) your feeling bubble "rest" and relax the muscles in your body. Repeat this cycle as many times as you like to explore the experience of giving this feeling your full attention while also being in charge of what this feeling is doing.

3. When your feeling bubble is as big as you choose it to be, visualize it moving *outside* of your body and *upward* until it is directly in front of your face.

4. Great! Now, with every exhale, imagine that the air leaving your nose (or mouth) is gently pushing the bubble away from you. With every inhale it "rests"; with every exhale it moves further away. Repeat a few times.

5. When you're satisfied with how far you've moved the feeling bubble, clap your hands and visualize it POP. Check in with your body and notice how you feel. Open your eyes and reconnect to where you are.

Do the best you can with this visualization, and feel free to peek at the steps if you get lost. You may want to record the steps on your phone for help staying on track. Give it a go and see how it feels.

Many girls notice that overseeing the expansion of the feeling (bubble) gives them a sense of power and authority over the feeling. Share what you noticed?

One takeaway is that even though you might feel powerless over difficult feelings, you can learn to focus, direct, and release any feeling you choose to work with.

NOTE OF ENCOURAGEMENT: If you have trouble visualizing, that's okay. Some people are naturally strong in this area while others get better with practice. It's best not to overthink whether you're doing it "right." Visualization is kind of like creating mental movies in your head, and if you like doing it, you can apply it to many different things in life. It's a mental health habit worth practicing.

SOUL SOOTHER: THE PHYSIOLOGICAL SIGH

Did you know that the average person sighs once every five minutes? That adds up to twelve sighs an hour! Since sighing is something you already do naturally, this soul soother may soon be a fave go-to anytime you feel stressed or overwhelmed. It was developed by neuroscientist Andrew Huberman. You can learn more about him from an internet search. (He has lots of interesting content about neuroscience and health.) If you'd like, you can even see him demonstrate this soul soother on YouTube (Huberman 2021). Try it out now:

- Inhale once through your nose, and when your lungs feel just about full, pause and follow up with another rapid inhale through your nose (two nose inhales).

- Exhale fully through your mouth, extending your exhale (one exhale).

- Repeat two to three times.

If, for any reason, it's uncomfortable to inhale through your nose, it's fine to inhale through your mouth. You've now enabled your body's relaxation response and added another bottom-up mental health habit to your list.

What did you notice?

If you'd like to make the physiological sigh a new go-to mental health habit, remember to write it on your favorites list.

CHAPTER 7

Free Yourself from Thinking Traps

Whether you think you can or you
think you can't, you're right.

—Henry Ford

The biggest change in my mental
health came when I learned not to
believe everything I think.

—Arial, age nineteen

 # LEARN

Since thoughts influence your feelings, and your feelings influence the actions you take (and don't take), improving your thinking habits goes a long way in improving your mental health. Thinking traps (aka *cognitive distortions*, or thinking mistakes) are flawed thinking habits that feed anxiety, lack of confidence, and a collection of other happiness killers. Thinking traps are extremely common and, if unchallenged, can make your life feel unbearable. Why do they exist? As you know, your brain has a lot to process all day long. To deal with the volume, it finds shortcuts to ease the processing burden. Unfortunately, faster doesn't mean better or more accurate, and thinking traps end up causing more harm than good.

  # REFLECT AND EXPLORE

Below is a list of common traps. Reflect and explore how you relate to each.

PERSONALIZING: Interpreting something as personally about you when it isn't. Example: Alina thinks her friends ditched her on purpose when she sees them together on social media.

If Alina were your sister or an upset friend of yours, how would you counsel her? Is there a way to validate her feelings without agreeing with her interpretation of what's going on?

Have you ever taken someone else's actions personally, only to find out later that there was another explanation that had nothing to do with you? What happened?

Full disclosure, to get you thinking about climbing out of traps, it helps to practice what you would say to a friend, because teen girls are often more loving and supportive to their friends than themselves. It's a way to practice the kind of loving support you will increasingly give yourself! To climb out of the personalizing trap, a great question to ask is *What if it's not personal? What's an alternative explanation?* Nine out of ten times, there's more to the story than what you can see when you're personalizing.

SHOULDING ON YOURSELF: Putting pressure on yourself by thinking you *should be* something you're not or that you *should do* something you haven't done. Unlike identifying ways you'd like to grow, *shoulding* has a judgmental energy that makes you feel bad—not encouraged. Example: Lexi's friends are taking driver's ed and are excited to drive. Lexi doesn't feel ready or interested. At the same time, she feels bad, constantly believing she should want to feel ready.

If Lexi were someone close to you, how would you support her? Reminder: When you start off by validating feelings, everything else you have to say works better.

_____

Do you *should* on yourself about anything, either past or present? What?

_____

_____

How had or does shoulding affect the way you feel and the actions you take or don't take?

_____

_____

The bottom line with shoulding is that it produces more negativity than productivity. If you want to stretch yourself, *encouragement* is much more motivating than shoulding.

FORTUNE-TELLING: Acting like you know what's going to happen when you actually can't be sure. Example: On the way to a social event, Ella says that she "knows" it will be stupid and a waste of her time. She wants to turn around and go home.

If you were in the car with Ella and wanted to help her out of this thinking trap, what would you say? (Remember to validate feelings first and find a ladder second.)

Can you think of a time when you did some fortune-telling? Are you doing it about anything currently? If so, share any insights you have about how this thinking trap affects you.

Bottom line on fortune-telling is that it's your mind jumping to an imagined version of the "truth," taking a shortcut instead of just being in the moment with an open mind and some optimism. This trap gets its power by convincing you that risk and uncertainty are intolerable and should be avoided at all costs—better to believe the worst and avoid it. A useful ladder out might involve helping Ella, or yourself, accept uncertainty, trusting that even if you're disappointed or uncomfortable, you can handle it and feel good about trying.

OVERGENERALIZING: Drawing a broad conclusion from insufficient evidence. Example: Sarah assumes that since her last friend group betrayed her confidence, girls can't be trusted. Even though this is a thinking trap, it feels to Sarah like there's a benefit (or upside) to it. She believes hanging on to the worst possible conclusion will keep her safe from further betrayal.

What about the downside to Sarah's overgeneralizing? What is this thinking mistake costing her?

Do you have a place in your life where you overgeneralize? Write about it including the upside and downside:

Helpful ladders for overgeneralizing might involve reminding a friend or yourself to be in the present moment and open to new possibilities. Additionally, you're always learning and growing, so if a similar situation presented itself, there's a good chance you'd navigate it with more clarity. You can be open and optimistic, while also reminding yourself to keep your eyes open for signs to navigate carefully.

ALL-OR-NOTHING THINKING: When you think in extremes, aka *black-and-white* thinking. Example: Maddie calls herself "a loser" when she doesn't catch on to things right away. If she's not "good" at something, she thinks she "sucks," as if there were only two categories and nothing in between.

How would you respond to Maddie if she were your friend? (Remember to validate feelings first before exploring a ladder out of this thinking trap.)

Think of an example of all-or-nothing thinking from your own life and write about it. What was or is the situation?

If you were to rethink the situation without all-or-nothing thinking, what would your new way of thinking be? (Hint: Explore opening your mind and heart.)

Next time you find yourself in all-or-nothing thinking, free yourself by coming up with more open-minded and open-hearted interpretations of what's going on. You will not only feel better but also make better decisions about what to do and how to handle the situation.

CATASTROPHIZING: Jumping to the worst conclusion is another very common trap. Your mind goes from 0 to 100 with a worst-case scenario. Example: Chandra's crush stopped texting. She's sure it's over and feels anxious and terrible.

If Chandra were a friend of yours, what might you point out to her?

What have you catastrophized in your life? Are you catastrophizing anything now?

There are subtle ways you may catastrophize that are harder to recognize because they're less dramatic. Here are three examples of *catastrophizing-lite*:

- Layla tends to keep her true personality under control when around friends because she catastrophizes what might happen if she were her full, authentic self with them.
- Emma wants to stop soccer because her critical coach has taken the fun out of it for her. She catastrophizes the impact leaving will have on her coach, her team, and her parents, so she stays.
- Rose is in a relationship she'd like to be out of but stays in it because she catastrophizes how hard the breakup would be.

Can you relate to any of these examples? Say more:

_____

_____

_____

_____

_____

_____

_____

_____

NOTE OF ENCOURAGEMENT: Here are some helpful affirmations for moments of discomfort: *I accept that growth can feel uncomfortable, and that's okay*, and *Discomfort isn't a reason to avoid what's right for me.*

Create something you could say to each girl that includes (1) validating feelings and (2) offering support that opens their mind to other (noncatastrophic) possibilities.

TO LAYLA:

TO EMMA:

TO ROSE:

The bottom line on catastrophizing is to remember that feelings are not facts. Thinking that discomfort = danger will trap you into avoiding opportunities to grow. You aren't here, in your life, to avoid all things uncomfortable. You are here to live your best life, which entails managing the discomfort that comes when you make powerful decisions that are best for *you!*

 **ELEVATE**

The better you can spot thinking traps, the faster you'll grab a ladder and climb right out. This trap log is your place to record one thinking trap (and ladder) each day for a week. It will accelerate your learning process so that trap detection becomes automatic for you!

THINKING TRAP LOG

Sunday	
Monday	
Tuesday	
Wednesday	
Thursday	
Friday	
Saturday	

Challenge: SILLY STRATEGIES FOR STUBBORN THOUGHTS

When it comes to taming stubborn thoughts, you may need extra support. This challenge requires an open mind and the willingness to get silly. Don't be fooled by the silliness, though. It's the secret ingredient that helps interrupt the negativity track your brain is on. Challenge yourself by exploring each one! (Heads-up: You may want to do this where no one can overhear you.)

Choose a stubbornly sticky thought to work with: one that holds you back and makes you miserable.

Write it down here: _____

Excellent! Now, try each of the strategies below:

TALK TO YOUR THOUGHT: *Thank you, thought, but you're definitely not helpful. I release you now.* Follow this up with three deep, slow breaths. With each long exhale, picture the thought moving further and further away from you.

RIDICULIZE THE THOUGHT: Yes, "ridiculize" is a made-up word, but it's going to help change the way your brain is perceiving your thought. Give each of these a try:

- Singing the thought as if you were starring in the worst opera ever.

- Repeating the thought in any and every ridiculous voice you can.

- Creating a story out of the thought that is so beyond dramatic that you end up wearing out the thought—and possibly laughing.

PICK A NEW AND IMPROVED THOUGHT: *I'm not here to be perfect. I'm going to focus on doing my best and that's all I can do. Everything else takes care of itself.*

NOTE OF ENCOURAGEMENT: Okay weirdo, feel proud. If these strategies feel absurd, good! You don't *want* to take thinking traps seriously. You want to free yourself, so you can move on with more productive thoughts that actually help you.

Which tip worked best for you? What might the value be?

≋ SOUL SOOTHER: SELF-HAVENING

Working with thinking traps goes a long way in helping you regulate your emotions. Unfortunately, there will still be plenty of times you feel stressed out and in need of some serious soothing. Conflicts with friends, homework overload, problems at home, feeling low and uninspired when it comes to the stressors facing teens, the list is *long*.

Self-havening is a tool developed by Ronald Ruden (2010) that draws upon the field of neuroscience to calm your nervous system. It involves practicing a series of actions you can perform on yourself to settle all kinds of anxiety. Here's what to do:

1. Cross your arms over your chest and rest your hands on the top of each shoulder. Move your hands in a downward motion from your shoulders to your elbows, like you are petting yourself in long, soothing strokes. Repeat for a minute or as long as you like.

2. Now, you're going to focus on the palms of your hands. Placing them together, move your palms back and forth together, as if you were washing your hands. Make the movements slow and thoughtful, really maximizing the contact your palms have with each other. Repeat for a minute or longer.

3. Now, bring your hands to your face and starting at your forehead, simply run your fingers down your face, however it feels comfortable. Notice how soothing that is. Repeat for about a minute.

That's it! The great thing about self-havening is that you can do all three steps or just one or two. Explore this technique next time you need some help regulating your anxiety or calming your stress.

How did it feel?

NOTE OF ENCOURAGEMENT: Self-havening is yet another new mental health habit you may want to add to your list of favorites. Many teens find that the more they practice self-havening, the more they feel the positive effects.

CHAPTER 8

Clean Out
Your Critic

"

Talk to yourself like you would
to someone you love.

—Brené Brown

"

"

Honestly, no one talks to me as
horribly as I talk to myself.

—Bella, age sixteen

 **LEARN**

Speaking kindly to your emotions is a form of positive *self-talk* that you've already worked on. Now it's time to address the inner chatter that never sleeps. It's another form of self-talk that, as you know, can be either helpful or absolutely treacherous.

You might be a fortunate teen whose self-talk tends to be comforting and encouraging. If this is you, you have a strong *inner comforter* that supports you throughout the day. More commonly, teens say they have an *inner critic* that's meaner to them than anyone they know. The inner critic is quick to point out all the ways you're messing up or falling short. Identifying this critic is important, because if you're absorbing a steady stream of emotional abuse all day, it takes a toll on your mental health.

 **REFLECT**

Some teens admit to having a downright hateful inner critic that stalks their every move with critical commentary. When they make a mistake or feel disappointed, they speak to themselves in a way they would never speak to another person. Other teens have a more encouraging way of talking to themselves through hard moments.

Do you talk to yourself like someone you love? When it comes to self-talk, what do you observe?

Place a heart along the scale to best represent where you are:

 ——————————————— ——————————————— ★

| I have a strong inner critic. | I have both, and they have equal power. | I have a strong inner comforter. |

If you have a strong inner critic, getting to know it will help you gain power. Do you know when it started? What age were you when you first noticed that critical inner voice?

Do you remember what was happening in your life at that time?

How did it affect the way you felt about yourself?

If you have a comforting voice, do you know when that started?

Does it sound like or remind you of anyone you know?

Think of a few times this comforting voice helped you out. Choose one of those times and write a few lines:

 **EXPLORE**

Being aware of your inner critic helps you slow down and separate your critic's take on things from a more helpful and realistic approach to whatever's going on. Unnoticed, your inner critic's perspective will simply feel like reality to you. You'll believe hurtful things about yourself that aren't even true—or that are a little true but are blown out of proportion, because inner critics exaggerate small flaws and failings.

To help you identify your inner critic, start by giving it a name. Remember the power of silliness? A ridiculous name is encouraged, since it will help you take your inner critic less seriously.

I'm naming my inner critic: _____

Give yourself a minute to draw your critic. Consider setting a timer and just scribble something quickly.

NOTE OF ENCOURAGEMENT: Once again, you are *turning toward* a mental health challenge, so you can get to know it and become more powerful. It's the things you deny or hide from that jump you from behind. Now let's dig into this little troublemaker.

Write about some situations that trigger your inner critic. Example: *When I meet someone new, and it takes me a while to warm up.*

What are some things it says when you make a mistake or fall short of your expectations? Write as many things as you can think of, so when they come up again in your head, you'll hear them for what they are and remember "who" is saying them.

Check in with your feelings by taking a long, slow breath and reading what you've written. Share any thoughts or feelings that come up for you:

_____

_____

_____

_____

_____

_____

_____

NOTE OF ENCOURAGEMENT: Sometimes when having a hard time, teens feel that they deserve to suffer the mean things their inner critic says to them. This just doesn't make sense. When you are having a hard time, even if you've "blown it" on a large scale, you need _more_ kindness, not less.

Imagine a person (real or made up) who does not intimidate you at all—in fact, they actually annoy you. How would you handle this person if they said the same things your inner critic says to you?

_____

_____

_____

_____

 **ELEVATE**

Imagine if a miracle happened in your sleep tonight and you woke up tomorrow morning changed forever. For some magical reason, your inner critic moved out of your head. Gone! Instead you notice only comforting self-talk. Imagine that deeply for a moment, and write about what changes because of this overnight miracle.

With others, I'd feel more

And probably act more

Just inside myself, I think I'd feel

In stressful moments, I wouldn't

Instead, I would

NOTE OF ENCOURAGEMENT: Some people feel that if they were truly kind and loving to themselves, they'd somehow become lazy or conceited. This is a mistaken belief. Just think of a great coach or teacher or person in your life who brings or has brought out the best in you. Are those people critical, or are they encouraging? Comfort and encouragement are much more powerful in bringing out the best in you. Make a clear commitment to stopping your inner critic in its tracks, over and over and over again. You can do it!

Challenge: CURL UP WITH YOUR INNER COMFORTER

While it would be amazing if your inner critic simply vanished overnight, that was a thought experiment to open your heart and mind. To replace your critic with your inner comforter, you'll need to develop a habit of switching your focus to give less attention to you-know-who. Makes sense, right? Whatever you focus on gets bigger.

For this challenge, fill every line below with the words of comfort and encouragement you'll offer yourself in times of need. If this challenge is hard for you, it's *even more* important that you stick with it. Growth comes through healthy struggle, so struggle away, and don't rest until the clouds are full:

How did that feel? What did you notice?

Can you commit to practicing comforting self-talk? What might the benefits be?

Name four situations in your life where you would most benefit from comforting self-talk:

To really sear this tip in, imagine one of those situations now, *but add comforting self-talk*. Visualization is always a great way to acquaint your brain with something you want it to learn and wire for. Take a few minutes to do this.

How did that feel?

NOTE OF ENCOURAGEMENT: Great work! Come back to this page when you need reminding and inspiration. When it comes to comforting and encouraging yourself, there's no such thing as too much.

PSYCH TIP: GET ARTSY

This tip is perfect for a day when your critic is on full blast. (Privacy recommended.)

You will need two supplies: a Band-Aid and a permanent marker. If you've got googly eyes on hand, excellent. Keep in mind that this tip is both powerful and ridiculous. Go with it. Wrap the Band-Aid around the index finger of your nondominant hand (the one you don't write with). With your finger facing you, draw a face on it. Give it as much detail as you can, and keep in mind that you're designing the face of your inner critic.

It's time for a little face-to-face with your critic whom, don't forget, you can call by name. Have it speak to you directly saying all the things it's been dishing out all day. Don't hold back. By taking the critic out of your head and into the open for a face-to-face, you're exposing your critic for what it is. Your critic is about as valid as the face on your finger trash-talking you.

Your conversation doesn't have to be one-way. Feel free to talk back, set boundaries, and advocate for yourself. In doing so, you're making yourself more powerful than this ridiculous hater, and showing that it's only as powerful as you allow it to be.

NOTE OF ENCOURAGEMENT: You just crushed two psych tricks: a pattern interrupt and externalizing the problem. A *pattern interrupt* is something you do to throw your brain off a negativity track. For example, you start singing very bad fake opera instead of throwing something across the room. You jump in a cold shower instead of doing something you'll regret. *Externalizing a problem* involves taking something that you think of as *you* and relating to it as if it were some kind of entity outside yourself (like a cartoon character or, in this case, an index finger with a Band-Aid on it). Externalizing gives you a break from feeling fused with the problem, so you can deal with it more effectively, as if it were a relationship that you're managing.

Good work! Many teens share that even if they do this exercise only once, this image of their inner critic sticks, allowing a permanent shift in power.

≋ SOUL SOOTHER: GET GROUNDED

Ever notice when you're anxious, you're in your head either stressing about the future or fretting about the past? Grounding exercises are a way to get out of your head, so you can reconnect to your body, your physical environment, and the present moment. There are many grounding exercises you can use to turn down stress and turn UP the calming response in your body. (Don't worry, you *do* have a calming response and it gets stronger the more you use it with the skills you're learning.)

Here's a grounding exercise that's both simple and effective.

Take yourself somewhere it's safe to walk barefoot. It could also be outside on the grass, sand, or whatever feels appealing underfoot where you are. At night or in cold weather, it might be a room in your home or a porch.

With your shoes off and no phone or other technology to distract you, spend two to five minutes (or more) walking, taking in the sites around you, feeling the air, and steering your mind back (again and again and again) to the present moment. If you have the time and the interest, lie down on the ground (or grass) and look up at the sky. Get a new visual perspective while feeling the earth supporting you. Notice where your body holds tension and see if you can soften those muscles. Take some lovely deep breaths as a gift to your nervous system. When you feel complete with this grounding exercise, give your body a nice stretch and go back to your life feeling more grounded. Give it a try!

What did you notice?

NOTE OF ENCOURAGEMENT: More than ever, teens talk about feeling overstimulated, robotic, empty, and anxious. Grounding exercises are an excellent way to drop into your body and the world around you. Feel free to stack on other habits that you've learned, such as deep breathing (making your exhale a little longer than your inhale), and comforting self-talk. Both of these habits are grounding too.

CHAPTER 9

Manage Anxiety Effectively

Where focus goes, energy flows.

—Tony Robbins

I feel like anxiety has more control
of my life than I do.

—Rachel, age fifteen

 **LEARN**

You're probably not surprised to hear that anxiety is a top mental health complaint among teens. While few things feel worse than feelings of dread, nervousness, and overwhelm, understanding how anxiety works and how to respond goes a long way in managing it down to size.

Believe it or not, not all anxiety is bad. If you are alive, you will certainly experience anxiety from time to time. At lower levels, it can be a sign that you're stretching out of your comfort zone and trying new things. Low levels of anxiety can also help you focus and get motivated. At higher levels, anxiety gets in the way of thinking clearly, being yourself, and connecting with people and opportunities. When symptoms of anxiety creep in—or hit hard—many girls have a strong urge to pull back and avoid whatever's triggering their uncomfortable feelings. While avoiding triggers for anxiety may offer short-term relief, it makes you more sensitive to anxiety in the long run.

 **REFLECT**

Now for some good news: you're in a great position to manage the hell out of anxiety. All the mental health habits you're *already* working on make you stronger and more resilient to all kinds of stress. For example, a lot of anxiety is a result of people being afraid of their feelings—but you're already on top of that. A lot of anxiety is due to poor thinking habits—but you're on top of that too! The more health you build, the less power anxiety has over you. But no getting lazy, because there's more work to do. Anxiety is one of those mental health challenges that requires *many different efforts*.

If you hear other people talking about their anxiety, and think to yourself how different it is from yours, it's because anxiety's symptom profile can vary greatly from person to person. Let's start by looking at your specific symptoms.

Think of anxiety as causing *neck up* and *neck down* symptoms. Neck up symptoms affect you mentally, while neck down symptoms affect you physically. Using these lists, identify the symptoms that affect you. Then represent them in the body outline with a 1 to 10 rating to indicate the intensity of each symptom for you:

NECK UP

_____ Racing thoughts   _____ Uncontrollable overthinking

_____ Heightened alertness   _____ Obsessive thoughts

_____ Difficulty concentrating

_____ Add your own _____

_____ Add your own _____

NECK DOWN

_____ Muscle tension

_____ Upset stomach

_____ Shortness of breath

_____ Sweating

_____ Trembling or shaking

_____ Racing heart

_____ Tiredness and fatigue

_____ Dizziness

_____ Tingling in hands or body

_____ Add your own

_____

_____ Add your own

Knowing your symptoms helps you notice, name, and accept them when they arise. Instead of feeling ambushed and scared, you can greet your symptoms like you greet your other feelings. (*Hey there. I see you. I feel you. You are my symptoms of anxiety. It's okay. I'm here for you, and there's no actual danger here.*) This reaction is a huge step because when you greet symptoms with calm—instead of fear—you prevent the onslaught of more anxiety. On the other hand, when you react to symptoms with fear, your brain interprets your fear as confirmation that you're in *actual danger.* Then it says, *Yikes! I want this body to survive, so I'm going to release a shit ton of cortisol and adrenaline to prepare her to flee or fight for her life!*

If you were in a life-or-death situation, these emergency chemicals would be helpful. But when you aren't in actual danger, they are useless. They're just trapped in your body to trigger your symptoms of anxiety.

Bottom line: While you can't always control feelings of anxiety, *you can always work with your reaction.* It's your reaction that either soothes or escalates the anxiety that you experience.

NOTE OF ENCOURAGEMENT: Exercise is a powerful and effective way to use up the adrenaline and cortisol that your brain dumps into your body. Next time you feel anxious, head for your sneakers and go for a walk. Other forms of movement that use up those chemicals include stretching or yoga, running, working out at the gym, or dancing in your room. Notice how you feel better as you draw upon those chemicals and burn through them. Exercise and anxiety go together like chicken soup for a bad cold.

What forms of exercise work best for you?

 **EXPLORE**

IMAGINE THIS IS THE NEW YOU: You feel good, most of the time. You have a lot of strong mental health habits and they're paying off. Since anxiety is part of life, you occasionally feel a flare-up. You know your symptoms well and feel a few firing up. In the old days, you would low-key panic over your symptoms. These days, you greet them much differently. While anxiety is uncomfortable, you know it's not dangerous, so you greet your symptoms calmly. You don't cancel your plans because avoidance isn't your go-to these days. You practice a breathing exercise to calm your nervous system, some soothing self-talk, and whatever self-care feels right in the moment.

ANXIETY AFFIRMATIONS: To direct your mind in a helpful way, practice these affirmations:

- *It's okay to be anxious. In this moment, I am completely okay.*
- *Anxiety in uncomfortable, not dangerous.*
- *It's okay to get triggered. I don't live in fear of my triggers.*
- *I can't eliminate triggers, but I can take control of my reaction.*
- *No one can see through me or read my mind. This is my personal experience, and I'm managing it.*
- *I'm not believing everything I think right now. I know anxiety causes my thoughts to be distorted.*
- *Feelings aren't facts. I'm holding everything lightly while I settle and reset my nervous system.*
- *It's totally fine to be uncomfortable. I accept my discomfort.*
- *I can be uncomfortable and still do what I want and need to do.*

For practice, personalize this experience of the new you with a paragraph of your own. Think of an anxiety flare-up you've had recently. Rewrite that experience from your new perspective. Include whatever triggered the anxiety (if you know) along with your symptoms. Choose one or more of your favorite ways to calm and soothe yourself, and write about how you made this work for you. As you explore the new you in this prompt, drop into the experience of *be*-ing the new and improved version of yourself. This will help you wire and create an improved response to anxiety when it arises.

 **ELEVATE**

While anxiety can seem to hit from out of the blue, there's often a trigger (aka *stressor*) that activates it. A relatively recent and widely held belief in our culture is that triggers should be avoided at all costs, and if someone has been extremely traumatized or is unwell, avoiding triggers may be necessary until they have a chance to get stronger. In general, however, expecting to avoid triggers for anxiety is unrealistic and unhelpful. As you've already learned, avoidance provides only short-term relief. When you avoid stressors that are not actually dangerous (when the danger is perceived versus actual), you become more sensitive to that stressor.

In some circumstances, triggers can be managed with healthy habits. For example, if being late is a trigger for anxiety, you can become a great time manager. If having a messy room is a trigger for your anxiety, you can prioritize keeping your room clean. If low blood sugar is a trigger for your anxiety, you can pack healthy snacks to have available. If you can't plan for a trigger that isn't actually dangerous, make friends with it. Get to know it. Increase your ability to experience it more calmly. Let's get to know your triggers and ways to respond.

Here are some examples:

TRIGGER: CONFLICT

(relationship problems, arguments, and disagreements)

Unhelpful responses:

Blowing up, shutting down, gossiping, blaming, avoidance, defensiveness

Helpful responses:

Direct communication, sharing feelings, listening, validating, apologizing, problem solving

TRIGGER: ACADEMIC STRESS

(worry about schoolwork, grades, test performance, college acceptance)

Unhelpful responses:

Procrastination, school avoidance, all-nighters, caffeine, skimping on sleep to get work done

Helpful responses:

Prioritizing schoolwork, good study habits, keeping up with assignments, asking for help, communicating with teachers, willingness to make changes in your course load and expectations

TRIGGER: SELF-NEGLECT

(not taking care of your physical body and emotions)

Unhelpful responses:

Denial, disinterest, avoidance, hopelessness, self-abandonment

Helpful responses:

Reconnecting with hydration, sleep, healthy meals, emotional check-ins, quality people and activities

TRIGGER: UNCERTAINTY

(not knowing how something will unfold or what will happen)

Unhelpful responses:

Obsessing, worrying, catastrophizing, avoiding

Helpful responses:

Creating a good plan, trusting yourself, trusting others, reminding yourself that you're safe

You may relate to one or more of the above triggers or have entirely different triggers. Reflect on your triggers and represent them in the boxes provided. Just write what comes to you.

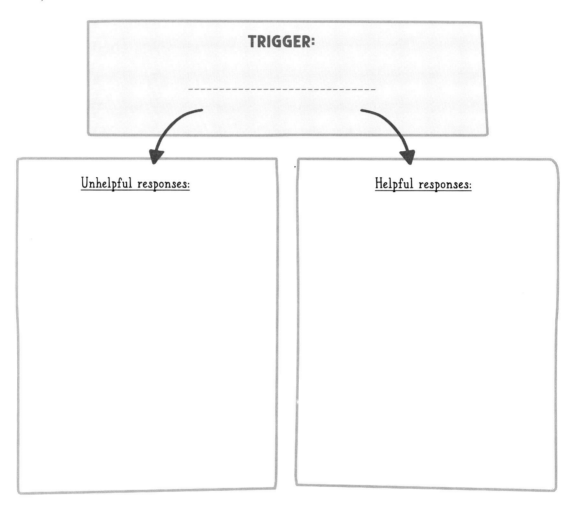

TRIGGER:

Unhelpful responses:

Helpful responses:

Along with everything you just learned about anxiety, keep in mind that sometimes you need to make changes in your *external life* to set yourself up for a more peaceful existence. In other words, you need to manage your *stressors* as well as your stress. For teen girls, a common stressor is a too-busy schedule or a not-busy-enough schedule. To elevate your mental health, good strategies are sometimes not enough. Set yourself up for success by making sure different elements of your life support your mental health. In the space below, record any external stressors in your life that need managing:

External stressor: | A change I can make:

Good work, now are you ready for your challenge? If you consider yourself a worrier, this one's for you!

Challenge: WORRY SMARTER

Worry is a thinking habit that causes a lot of anxiety. It constitutes thoughts that range from nagging concerns to intense preoccupation about what *might* happen. When it takes over your thoughts, you may experience sleeplessness, feelings of doom, an inability to eat, and the whole array of anxious symptoms. Ugh, why?!?

Like many bad mental health habits, worry has good intentions. At some point in your life, your brain decided that worrying was a productive activity. Most likely because you didn't like feeling surprised, vulnerable, or out of control, your brain stepped in with a "solution."

I've got a great idea! If I work really hard to anticipate any/every bad thing that could happen, I can catch things ahead of time and prepare for them. Or avoid them! Nothing will ever scare me or surprise me again because I will see it coming! What a great idea! This is going to be super helpful and productive.

What your brain didn't realize is that every time you imagined a scary or upsetting scenario to worry about, another part of your brain reacted by releasing stress hormones to prepare you for action. If you were in *real danger*, those chemicals would help you to run or fight. Since worry involves *perceived danger* (not in-the-moment actual danger), those stress chemicals stay in your body, causing symptoms of anxiety.

Seems like any habit that causes so much suffering should be immediately squashed, right? Suppressing thoughts and feelings never works, which is why you're working on noticing, naming, and accepting all your thoughts and feelings. From there, you're practicing finding where feelings are in your body, attending and befriending them, and eventually redirecting your focus and actions in a healthy way. You're building a solid foundation and are ready for a new mental health habit designed specifically for worry!

128

For this challenge, you are asked to designate fifteen minutes each day to actually dedicate to worrying. That's right, it's counterintuitive, but it works! Just as you'd tell a friend or a family member, "Hey, I can't talk about that now. It's not helpful," you'll make a similar boundary with worry thoughts. (Yes, you can make boundaries with your thoughts!)

When worries pop up at other times during the day or night, you'll notice, name, and accept that they're happening. Then you'll make your boundary, letting them know they must wait until the next designated time of day for worrying. Be firm, as if you were babysitting a small child pestering you for a brownie before lunch. Once you've said no, carry on with a more productive focus.

Your designated worry time can change each day, depending on your schedule. Make sure it's not first thing in the morning or before bed, and make sure to be strict with stopping yourself at a fifteen-minute time limit. During worry time, write down every worry thought that pops into your head. Think of it as purging your mind of every worry thought, removing worries from your head and relocating them onto the paper. When you are done, pause. Take a nice, deep breath, making the exhale just a little longer than your inhale.

Now, look at your list more objectively. Cross out any items that seem insignificant, or that you realize don't have much weight. For the remaining ones, decide whether there is an action you can take or a plan you can make to address or resolve the worry.

For example, Erika addressed her worry about going back to school after a breakup: "I was worried about how to handle seeing my ex and how things might feel awkward in our mutual friend group. So, I made a plan to walk onto campus being my normal self. No matter how my ex acted, I planned to say hello to show both him and my friend group that it didn't have to be weird. As soon as I made that plan and even visualized it, I felt better."

This challenge is so effective, you can practice it for life! To get you started, use the worry sheets that follow. After you use them up, you can start a notebook or even a note in your phone, dedicated to worrying smarter.

WORRY SHEET

List your worries here:

List your plans here:

DON'T FORGET YOU ONLY HAVE FIFTEEN MINUTES TO WORRY!

NOTE OF ENCOURAGEMENT: If you're not a regular worrier, skip this challenge or tailor it to your needs. For example, if you worry during finals, but you don't worry much other than that, schedule worry during finals. When you notice you're going through a stressful time, schedule worry to free your mind at other times.

PSYCH TIP: CLARIFY YOUR CIRCLE OF POWER

This psych tip is so life changing, it will change the way you navigate stress forever. Once you've got it down, you'll economize your energy by training your focus *toward what you can control* and *away from what you can't.*

As you know, you face challenges and stressors every day. Some you can do something about. Some you can't. Clarifying the difference helps you focus on what you can control and to accept what you can't, without overthinking everything to death and making yourself miserable. Ready to clarify your circle of power? Here you go.

Imagine a circle surrounding you. Inside the circle are all the things in your life that you have control over: things you can impact. Outside the circle are all the things you don't have control over: things you may be able to *influence*, but that's as far as your power goes. Sad as it may be, you just don't have ultimate control over things outside your circle.

Here's an example:

While you can't completely control your grade, you can try to influence it by focusing your energy on everything inside the circle. Sure, the teacher may give you an insane test with material you haven't even learned yet, or you could feel sick or exhausted that day, due to factors outside your control.

My chem grade

Studying for my exams.
Keeping up with homework.
Asking for help.
Getting more sleep.
Making flash cards.
Setting up a study group.

Getting clear on what you do and do not have power over helps you train your mind to focus on life inside your circle. When your focus strays (and gets stuck) on things outside your circle, you practice noticing, naming, accepting, exploring the feelings in your body and saying hello to them, and then firmly guiding your attention back to everything inside the circle.

As you consider the items inside your circle, check in with yourself to see if you need to take any action. If there's action to take, access your self-confidence and self-discipline, and take action. If no action is required, train yourself to accept that no action can be taken, and switch your focus to something more productive or enjoyable.

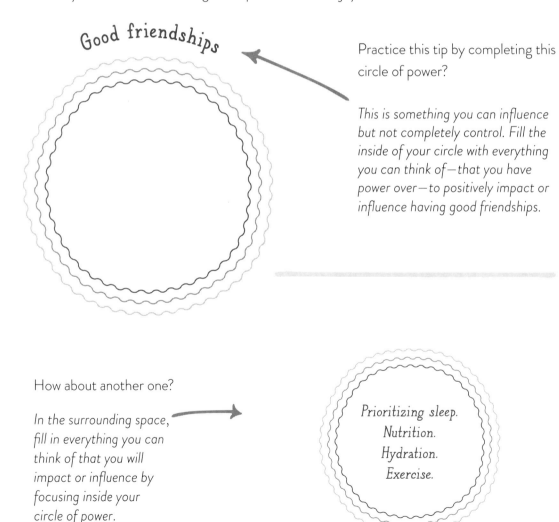

Good friendships

Practice this tip by completing this circle of power?

This is something you can influence but not completely control. Fill the inside of your circle with everything you can think of—that you have power over—to positively impact or influence having good friendships.

How about another one?

In the surrounding space, fill in everything you can think of that you will impact or influence by focusing inside your circle of power.

Prioritizing sleep.
Nutrition.
Hydration.
Exercise.

This one is all yours. Think of a struggle or source of stress you have in your life (past, present, or future) and fill in everything you can think of that's inside—and outside—your circle of power.

NOTE OF ENCOURAGEMENT: Great practicing. When you get comfortable with this skill, you'll find yourself applying it *in the moment*. Once you've clarified where to take action, you can empower yourself to influence the outcomes you'd like and let go of what you cannot control.

Speaking of letting things go...

≋ SOUL SOOTHER: AFFIRMATIONS FOR LETTING GO

What a perfect time for more affirmations, because sometimes letting go of things outside your circle of power is easier said than done.

Read each affirmation and then close your eyes and repeat either aloud or silently.

I can only do what I can do. I let go of the rest.

_____

I accept the things I can't control.

_____

My focus is everything inside my circle of power.

_____

No matter how things unfold, I'll be okay.

_____

Remember how there's an additional layer of soothing when you write? Go ahead and write each soothing affirmation on the line underneath it, and just notice yourself as you deeply absorb its meaning.

Add your own affirmation here if you'd like: _____

_____

_____

POP QUIZ: UNHEALTHY HABITS

You're doing a beautiful job focusing on mental health habits that promote and sustain strong mental health, but what about unhealthy habits you may have that you're attached to—meaning, you'd prefer not to give up? Or maybe you've tried to give them up, but it's harder than you thought.

Here is a list of common mental health habits that work *against* your big picture health and well-being. Check off any of these that you use to any degree, and make notes about your relationship with the habit: how big of a problem is it, how long has this been a habit, and what are the upsides and downsides of this habit as you see or experience it? Be honest with yourself. "Massaging" the truth may be helping you maintain an unhealthy behavior that works against your big picture happiness, health, and freedom.

○ **VAPING**

_____

_____

○ **RESTRICTING FOOD (OR BINGEING)**

_____

_____

○ **SHOPLIFTING**

_____

_____

○ **EXCESSIVE SOCIAL MEDIA** (trust your gut with what "excessive" means to you)

_____

_____

○ **SELF-HARMING BEHAVIORS**

_____

_____

○ **NEGLECTING SLEEP**

_____

_____

- **IMPULSIVE DECISION MAKING** (sexual hook-ups, unsafe driving, reckless decisions about physical or emotional safety)

- **AVOIDING OPPORTUNITIES TO GROW**

- **RAGING** (aka angry outbursts)

- **SUBSTANCE USE**

- **EXCESSIVE GAMING**

- **SOCIAL WITHDRAWAL** (hiding from the world)

What feelings came up for you in this exercise? If you felt irritated, defensive, anxious, or resistant, that's understandable. Make sure to write about feelings and not thoughts.

What thoughts came up for you in this exercise? Defensive thoughts, such as *This is stupid*, along with the urge to rush through or skip this section, are completely human. Part of you may want to protect a habit you're attached to, even though you know it's not the best.

Being totally honesty here, what impact does this habit or do these habits have in these areas?

YOUR MENTAL HEALTH:

FEELINGS ABOUT YOURSELF:

RELATIONSHIPS WITH OTHERS:

If you were to stop or replace the habit or behavior with a better one, what difficulties (social, emotional, practical) might you encounter?

How might you handle those difficulties? Is there anything you've learned in this journal that you could use to support you?

Are you assuming the habit or behavior will get better on its own or fade with time? Is that realistic or is it a way of avoiding what's true?

Do you need adult support? Who can you go to?

What can you do or not do about this habit that will most benefit you six months from now? A year from now?

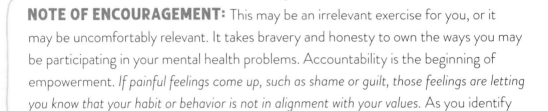

NOTE OF ENCOURAGEMENT: This may be an irrelevant exercise for you, or it may be uncomfortably relevant. It takes bravery and honesty to own the ways you may be participating in your mental health problems. Accountability is the beginning of empowerment. *If painful feelings come up, such as shame or guilt, those feelings are letting you know that your habit or behavior is not in alignment with your values.* As you identify habits that work against you, even if they feel good in the moment, you can empower yourself to make important changes. You are worth it!

⭐ MOOD TIPS FROM TEENS ⭐

Syd, age nineteen: *"I knew for eight months that I needed to stop vaping, before I finally made a boundary with myself. When I started, it wasn't a big deal for me, but over time I began to feel more anxious, hit my vape more, and the vicious cycle began. When I was home for spring break, I told my parents. It was a relief for me because it was hard to hide, and they could tell something was going on with me because I was so freaking annoyed and short all the time. I thought it was just me or that they were more annoying than before, but it was the nicotine and my addiction to it. It was not a fun conversation, but they did support me and I've been nicotine free for four months."*

CHAPTER 10

Nurture Healthy Relationships

> The only way to have a friend
> is to be one.
> —Ralph Waldo Emerson

> I haven't always had the best luck
> with friends and it's hurt me a lot.
> —Gaby, age fourteen

🍃 LEARN

As a teen girl, your relationships can be a source of some of your greatest happiness and your deepest pain. When things are good, relationships (friends, family, and significant others) can be the fun secure heart of your existence. Wanting connection, acceptance, and a feeling of security with your people isn't random; it's deeply embedded in your human design. In our evolution, being in groups with other humans had strong survival value.

But relationships aren't always easy. When challenges arise, you might feel confused, anxious, and unsure about how to handle things. Your parents' generation didn't have to deal with the stress of seeing friends hanging out without them on social media or significant others "liking" sexy posts of other girls.

Then there's feeling like you're being talked about, dealing with friends acting "different" and not knowing why, and various flavors of drama that either involve you or affect you. You may get advice to just talk it out and say how you feel, but teen girls often hold back in fear of an unpredictable outcome.

Good thing you know about your circle of power, because it comes in handy again and again in life. Instead of getting stuck in endless overthinking about relationship dynamics, you can build a habit of focusing on things you can control *inside your circle of power*. If you can't control them, you strengthen a habit of letting them go and reallocating your focus in a healthier direction.

Why is this a solid plan? Because you can only control yourself. When you focus on everything inside your circle of power, you set yourself up for relationship health and success. While you can't control other people (outside the circle), you can absolutely feel clear about habits that nurture relationships *inside* your circle of power. Let's jump inside that circle and do some exploring.

 **REFLECT**

How do you see your current relationship habits? Place a heart on the scale below that best represents you:

I'm not sure
what good
habits are.

I have some good
and bad habits.

I think I'm good at
relationships and
have solid habits.

What kind of experiences have you had in relationships?

I've had some
really hurtful
experiences.

I've had a few
hard experiences
but mainly good.

I've had mostly
good experiences
in relationships.

What are a couple of qualities you bring to your relationships that you're proud of? (These might be things like good listening, fun, empathy, compassion, thoughtfulness.)

_____

_____

_____

What positive relationship feedback have you received from others about what they appreciate about you?

_____

_____

_____

Are there ways you'd like to become better in relationships? Name a few ways you'd like to grow or improve your relationship habits:

What are the top ten things you value in a friend or other relationship?

1.

2.

3.

4.

5.

6.

7.

8.

9.

10.

 **EXPLORE**

Let's explore some healthy relationship habits and look at your strengths in each of these areas, along with areas where you can improve, so you can feel strong inside your circle of power. Remember, self-acknowledgement is important, so make sure to pause and feel positive about your good social habits. Open your heart to any weaknesses because *you're not here to be perfect.* Identifying areas in need of improvement, without denial, defensiveness, or excessive shame, is a sign of emotional maturity that many adults lack! (You've seen it, and it's not pretty.) Feel good about your willingness to do hard things.

RADIATING OUT

Knowing how to radiate your personal energy out to others is a habit that may or may not come naturally. Gestures such as offering eye contact, a friendly smile, a warm hello, and a heartfelt compliment have a bigger impact on your social life than you may realize. Most people respond favorably to warm social gestures and return the energy back to the giver, no matter how indifferent they may appear. When you radiate warm energy as you walk through the hall or into a room, you let people know: *I'm kind. I'm confident. I see you. I'm accessible. I'm someone you can also acknowledge.*

NOTE OF ENCOURAGEMENT: Most communication is *nonverbal.* When you pass by or meet someone you like or feel good around, it's seldom about their verbal communication and *much more* about their energy. Notice people who exude what you'd like to exude. Notice people who seem curled into themselves, as if they wanted to take up as little space as possible or be invisible. Which is more inviting?

When it comes to radiating out, what do you see about yourself? What are your strengths and weaknesses? (Here *weakness* = something *not yet developed*, not something you can't change.)

STRENGTHS

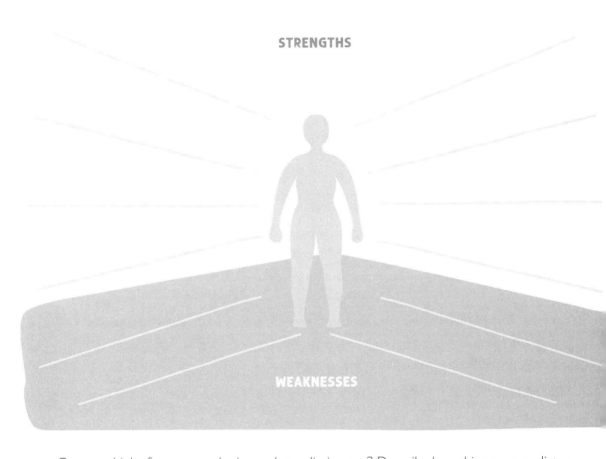

WEAKNESSES

Can you think of someone who is good at radiating out? Describe how this person radiates good vibes, what you observe, and how it feels to you.

COMMUNICATE MINDFULLY

A lot of intimacy in relationships is created through light chatting, deeper sharing, and always, always, *good listening*. The better a person listens (without judging or switching the focus to themself or another topic), the more they offer to the person sharing. When people think of someone in their life that they feel closest to, they often describe that person as a good and caring listener.

But there's more, and you may be better at one than the other. Opening up to others, in healthy ways, creates intimacy. Think of people with whom you feel close. It's usually not a surface relationship, but one with more depth and sharing. On the other hand, when people share too much, too soon, others may feel overwhelmed or burdened, leaving the sharer feeling emotionally unsafe and overexposed.

When it comes to sharing with others:

- *I'm guarded. Sharing isn't easy.*

- *I'm open, but don't share personal stuff until trust is established.*

- *Before I know it, I overshare and end up feeling cringey about it.*

Do certain experiences come to mind?

When it comes to listening:

- *I have a hard time listening.*

- *I listen but bring the conversation back to me.*

- *I must be a great listener because I'm the "therapist" for my friends.*

What experiences come to mind?

Who in your life is easiest to talk to? What qualities of this person make opening up possible?

Have you been or are you in the position of "therapist" to a friend or friends? What's that like for you? Describe the upsides or downsides of that role.

Being the therapist for one or several friends means you may miss out on being seen for all of who you are, and it can also be a big responsibility. If you feel anxious about your friend's mental or physical health and safety, or if your friend is engaging in self-harm or other risky behaviors, it's time to reach out to an adult, like a parent, grandparent, teacher, or school counselor. As big as your heart is, you're not a professional, and taking on the responsibility for the mental health of another person is too much for you. Have you ever been in this position, or are you now?

BRINGING POSITIVITY

When life feels hard, it's easy to fall into a negativity trap. While a certain amount of venting and complaining is understandable, too much focus on everything that sucks is unhealthy for everyone. Especially in times of stress, focusing on tiny joys and small pleasures is a very healthy habit in relationships. Reflecting on yourself, what do you see?

- *I tend to get stuck in negativity.*

- *I can always find things that I enjoy or that I'm grateful for.*

- *I feel like I fake happiness to keep others happy (or because I think that they expect it from me).*

Say more about the circle you checked. What feelings come up for you? Is there an upside or a downside?

Are there any changes you'd like to make that would feel better and be healthier for you? For your relationships?

If you *perform*, or fake happiness to keep others happy, how is that for you? Is it a burden? How does it feel? Can you imagine making changes in that habit? Where could you start and what might you begin to do a little differently?

NOTE OF ENCOURAGEMENT: If you perform happiness, you may be *catastrophizing* what would happen if you stopped. (*I'll lose my value. People will see the real me. I'll let people down. People need me to be sunny all the time.*) It could be that you have a self-limiting belief that's getting in the way of feeling more genuine. No one's happy all the time, and it's not your job to provide the world its sunshine.

Thoughts or feelings?

THOUGHTFULNESS AND CONSIDERATION

Remembering to check in about a friend's sick grandma, sticking to plans instead of being flaky, remembering to be present instead of distracted by your phone—these are all examples of showing thoughtfulness and consideration in relationships. What's your experience in this department?

PERSONALLY:

◯ I get in my own head a lot and am not that thoughtful or considerate.

◯ I try to remember to keep my friends' lives and needs on my radar.

◯ I give too much to my relationships. I wish they were more even.

WITH OTHERS:

◯ I wish others were as thoughtful with me as I am with them.

◯ I experience a mix of hits and misses in my relationships.

◯ I have a lot of relationships that offer me thoughtfulness and consideration.

What or who came to mind as you checked the circles above? What thoughts and feelings or examples?

If something could change for the better, what would it be? Can you think of a way to make that change or ask for it?

SETTING HEALTHY BOUNDARIES

Communicating what's okay with you and what isn't creates the safety, respect, and trust required to build a healthy relationship. Same goes for honoring the boundaries of others. Many teen girls share that setting boundaries is hard because they don't want people to think they're a bitch or making a big deal about something. Reflecting on boundaries, what do you see in yourself?

- *I have a hard time setting boundaries. It stresses me out.*

- *I'm direct about sharing my boundaries.*

- *I sometimes find myself pushing the boundaries of others.*

What comes to mind as you reflect on the box you checked? What thoughts, feelings, or experiences come to mind? Any challenges?

_____

_____

_____

Is there a boundary you haven't made, but would like to? If so, fill in the blanks:

I'd like to/need to make a boundary with _____

about _____.

[describe the behavior that bothers you]

Choose an approach below to practice communicating a boundary with this person. Keep in mind your tone and firmness will vary depending on who the person is as well as the situation. If it's someone close to you who you know has no intention to harm you, you'll probably want to adopt a gentle approach, giving the person the benefit of the doubt. If it's someone not close to you and their behavior is unacceptable, you will probably want to be firmer.

Examples for how to phrase a boundary:

I know you would never intentionally hurt my feelings or make me uncomfortable, but I don't like it when you _____ .

[describe the behavior]

Or...

It doesn't work for me when you _____ .

[describe the behavior]

I ask that you _____ *instead.*

[say what you'd like them to do]

Or...

I've asked you not to _____ .

[describe the behavior]

Next time I will _____ .

[say what you will do to take care of yourself, such as leave, take space, ask for help, involve adults]

Think of a person and situation from your life, and practice boundary setting in the space below:

_____

_____

_____

_____

ELEVATE

Because you're human *and* a teenager, you know about harmful habits that threaten the health and happiness of relationships. Write about your experience with the following habits:

GOSSIPING. The most common harmful habit teen girls talk about is gossip. The challenging thing about this habit is that when you're struggling with one friend, venting or processing with another friend can feel necessary, even irresistible. As you may know, even when you think it won't get back to the friend you're struggling with, it often does. Now, on top of the original struggle, you've unintentionally created tension within multiple relationships because you now feel betrayed by the friend who broke your trust. This is just one example of how sensitive information often slips out without the intention to harm and things just get complicated.

Write about a personal experience (as either the *gossiper* or the *gossipee*). Include thoughts and feelings and how things unfolded—anything that comes to you.

Did any learning or growth come from that situation? For you or others? Or was there an end in the relationship?

_____

_____

_____

_____

COMPETING. Competing pops into relationships in different ways. Here are some examples: You're having a hard time, and when you tell a friend, they make a point of letting you know they're having a worse time. You've got some fun plans coming up, but you think your friend's plans are "better." Or more toxically, you've got a crush, and suddenly your friend is chatting up your crush.

Have you experienced competition in any of your relationships? Write about that experience, how it felt, and how things unfolded.

_____

_____

_____

Are there any takeaways or life lessons that you see for yourself or anyone involved? Did you learn anything that will help in the future?

_____

_____

_____

CONTROLLING. There are many ways control shows up in a friendship. It may be someone needing to get their way and failing to compromise or even check in with other people's preferences. Someone being possessive to control outside "threats" to a relationship. Someone forcing their opinions or values without respect for personal differences. Someone taking over the conversation or needing to be the center of attention. Someone deciding who is welcome and who isn't, without regard for other people's input. Are there ways you are controlling or have experience in dealing with controlling friends or significant others? Write about that situation and how you're feeling about it.

Is there anything you did or can do to improve this situation? Is there anything anyone did or could do to improve it?

SELF-ABSORPTION. When people are struggling or just haven't matured yet, they tend to be less thoughtful or considerate and more self-absorbed, talking and thinking mainly about themselves.

Is self-absorption a habit of anyone you know? Write about what comes to mind and any thoughts/feelings/examples or memories that come up for you.

Are there times when you feel stuck in self-absorption? Are there circumstances that trigger it? Do you have ways of shifting out of it?

 ## Challenge: TWO-DAY GOSSIP CLEANSE

For this challenge, explore cleansing negative comments about other people for forty-eight hours. Other people include:

- Parents, siblings, family members
- Teachers and coaches
- Acquaintances and strangers
- Current and past friends
- Current and past significant others

Instead of saying: *My coach was a crazy bitch today.* Switch to this: *My coach worked us hard today.* Instead of saying: *Once again, Emma is choosing her boyfriend over us this weekend.* Upgrade to: *Emma cancelled plans this weekend.*

By sticking to objective information and eliminating judgment-drenched commentary, you are cleansing gossip.

★ **EXTRA CREDIT CHALLENGE:** Here's a concept: include yourself in the gossip cleanse. You've already learned about your inner critic, self-limiting beliefs, and negative self-talk. What if you decided to *stop talking negatively about yourself*? No putting yourself down to others, no beating yourself up when you make a mistake... Absolutely no self-hate. Ever. Now *that* would be life changing! Any thoughts?

NOTE OF ENCOURAGEMENT: This is a two-day challenge for a reason. Most people are unaware of how pervasive their gossiping habit is. This cleanse requires committed self-awareness and self-monitoring to execute properly, which is hard!

After your two-day gossiping cleanse, come back to this section and write about what it felt like. How did it go? Any surprises? How did it feel? How hard was it?

Good work! Teen girls consistently report that even after this challenge has ended, they're more conscious of their gossip.

PSYCH TIP: NEITHER ABOVE NOR BELOW

Social comparison is as painful as it is common. Most teens say comparing themselves to others kicks in when they're around another girl or girls with whom they feel "less than." It's not always the clearly conscious thought *I feel less* _____ *than she is.* More often it presents as a feeling of being *not good enough.*

Social comparison can also present in the opposite direction. You may find yourself comparing yourself to other girls in a way that places you above or "better than" them. Girls who have this habit are often grasping for ways to feel more secure in themselves.

Social comparison is an unhelpful and often automatic habit that can be softened by the following exercise. With everyone you see, repeat this phrase silently: *I am neither above you nor below you. No matter how things appear, we're more the same than different.*

As much as you can, repeat that silent mantra throughout your day. Soak in the words and their meaning, not just with your head but with your heart. Teen girls consistently report feeling skeptical before practicing this tip, but guess how they feel afterward?

Better! Relieved! Social comparison is both exhausting and misleading, because humans are endlessly complex and judgments are grossly oversimplified. Additionally, the energy you generate when you compare yourself tends to be critical, negative, and anxious. These are not the vibes of your best mental health! Just practice recognizing and redirecting. Over time, your habits rewire your brain to be less negative.

Is there someone in your life with whom you have a lot of conflict? Here's a tip: think of them or picture them and practice your new mantra over and over. Notice how directing your thoughts affects the feelings in your body. Give it a try and write about what you notice.

～～ SOUL SOOTHER: CREATE PEACE AND BEAUTY

Have you ever noticed yourself feeling better when your personal space is organized and uncluttered? You're not alone. If your room is best described as "less than tranquil," you're missing out on a soul-soothing space to calm your mind and encourage a good night's sleep. As self-care for your soul, here are ideas shared by other teen girls.

ZAYA: "I share a room with my little sister—not great, obviously. We have an agreement that she stays away from my designated area. I was actually messier than her, until recently when I realized I couldn't sleep because my room felt so out of control. So, I got my closet under control first, and got rid of everything I don't like or that doesn't fit. Weirdly, that improved my mood more than I would have expected. I would say that, overall, I just feel better—like my room is a representation of my brain or something. I even make my bed every day, which is something I saw on social media for depression. It's not wrong: it's like I'm giving myself a message that I care when I make my bed. So, yeah, that's it."

IZZY: "My best friend's mom always has flowers at their house, and I always feel good being there. When I complimented the flowers one day, she gave me one in a little glass jar to take home, and I put it in my room. It's such a small thing, but it really changed the way I felt in my room and inspired me to make it nicer. Mostly I just put my clothes away and everything stays reasonably calm. Whenever I can, I clip a flower or even a little branch of something and put it in my vase. It makes me happy."

SOPHIA: "I saw someone on social media say, 'Leave it the way you want to find it,' and for some reason, it got in my head. Every time I feel like being lazy and throwing my clean clothes on the floor to fold later, I just say, 'F-it, do it now' and then I do it. Now I like to be in my room. A clean room is good for my mental health because I feel less lazy, I can find shit, I feel calmer and, I guess, proud—or maybe it's more like self-respect—and just less stressed, I think."

Write about anything in these thoughts that you can relate to.

What is the current state of your room? If you could make a change, or changes, to soothe your soul and lift your mood, what would it be?

Is there anything soulful you can add to your personal space? Personal art? Photos? Flowers or something from nature that speaks to your soul?

✹ MOOD TIPS FROM TEENS ✹

Ellie, age fifteen: *"You can tell how I'm doing by how my room looks. When I'm good and on track, my room is clean. When I'm a mess, usually because I'm procrastinating and low-key freaked out about it even though I'm not doing anything, my room is a mess. It's a vicious cycle, because then I get even more depressed. I'm getting better at putting on music and putting my clothes away. It's only a ten-minute thing if I do it a few times a week, and it's literally insane how much better I feel. It's like my life is manageable when my room is clean."*

CHAPTER 11

Get to Know Your Parts

> We don't realize that, somewhere within us all, there does exist a supreme self who is eternally at peace.
>
> —Elizabeth Gilbert

> Sometimes I feel like a low-key multiple personality. I can feel so many different ways about the same thing—it's a lot!
>
> —Nikki, age sixteen

 **LEARN**

Do you ever notice yourself feeling two (or more) completely different ways about the same topic? One part of you really wants to keep up with schoolwork, but another part wants to escape into distraction and avoidance. One part of you is eager for freedom and independence, but another part feels scared to grow up. One part of you loves your best friend, but another part feels extremely annoyed by her. One part of you wants to feel better, but another part wants to collapse into hopelessness.

Or maybe you notice *intense parts* that seem to come out of nowhere and take over your personality. For example, a sad part welling up inside you when you think you "should be" having a good time. Or an angry part that bursts out of you that feels beyond your control. Or an anxious part that goes silent (or becomes a "chatterbox") around people you're not comfortable with.

Psychologist Richard Schwartz (2018) writes about different "parts" that comprise who we are. These parts are like little beings inside of us with different thoughts, feelings, perspectives, and needs; no one is a completely coherent whole but more the sum or many different parts—and that's normal! This approach to therapy, known as internal family systems, or IFS, helps people get to know their parts, for growth and healing. Schwartz is clear that all your parts make sense, even when they seem to be a problem. For example, a perfectionist part of you may want to protect you from criticism or feeling "not good enough." An angry part may want to protect you from feeling hurt, scared, or vulnerable. A hurt part may want you to hide from challenges, to protect you from feeling overwhelmed.

 REFLECT

Let's get you thinking about different parts of yourself.

Take a look at the following list of parts that people often identify in themselves. You are completely unique, of course, so you may relate to some of these and not others. **Next to each part, give a 1 to 10 rating signifying how strongly you feel this part inside of you (1 = not at all, 10 = very strongly).** Then see if you can identify the good intention each part may have, and write it down. Even if it's a part you don't relate to, you may see it in others and be able to imagine the positive intention. There's no universal definition for these parts, so if you're not sure what "the Magical Child" or some other part is, just decide what it means *to you*, because that's all that matters. Write the good intention beside each part. Here are some examples:

✦ **THE COMPETITOR.** Rating: 8. Intention: Tries to help me feel good enough.

✦ **THE BITCH.** Rating: 5. Intention: It shows up when I need to protect myself or let people know they need to back off.

✦ **THE RISK TAKER.** Rating: 1. Intention: Probably makes people feel alive or brave. Maybe it wants to protect them from feeling their feelings or being sad.

✦ **THE PLEASER.** Rating: _____ Intention: _____

✦ **THE PERFECTIONIST.** Rating: _____ Intention: _____

✦ **THE COMPETITOR.** Rating: _____ Intention: _____

✦ **THE WOUNDED CHILD.** Rating: _____ Intention: _____

✦ **THE PLAYFUL CHILD.** Rating: _____ Intention: _____

✦ **THE SCARED CHILD.** Rating: _____ Intention: _____

✦ **THE CREATIVE CHILD.** Rating: _____ Intention: _____

✦ **THE QUEEN.** Rating: _____ Intention: _____

✦ **THE SHY ONE.** Rating: _____ Intention: _____

✦ **THE ATTENTION SEEKER.** Rating: _____ Intention: _____

✦ **THE ACHIEVER.** Rating: _____ Intention: _____

✦ **THE RISK TAKER.** Rating: _____ Intention: _____

✦ **THE VICTIM.** Rating: _____ Intention: _____

✦ **THE GOLDEN CHILD.** Rating: _____ Intention: _____

✦ **THE BITCH.** Rating: _____ Intention: _____

✦ **THE AVOIDER.** Rating: _____ Intention: _____

✦ **THE DREAMER.** Rating: _____ Intention: _____

✦ **THE MAGICAL CHILD.** Rating: _____ Intention: _____

✦ **THE LOVING CHILD.** Rating: _____ Intention: _____

✦ **THE ADVENTURER.** Rating: _____ Intention: _____

✦ **THE CARETAKER.** Rating: _____ Intention: _____

✦ **THE PROTECTOR.** Rating: _____ Intention: _____

✦ **THE REBEL.** Rating: _____ Intention: _____

✦ **THE ARGUER/FIGHTER.** Rating: _____ Intention: _____

Anything you don't see here that you'd like to add? The preceding list is far from complete or applicable to every person. Trust what comes to you.

✦ _____ Rating: _____ Intention: _____

✦ _____ Rating: _____ Intention: _____

NOTE OF ENCOURAGEMENT: Recognizing the parts that pop up in your life, and what they're trying to do, can help you open your heart to yourself and understand yourself better. When a challenging part pops up or stirs deeply inside you, explore noticing it with appreciation for its good intentions. It doesn't define you, but it's *a part of you* that needs your love and understanding. It may even need you to "parent" it a little: for example, a shy part may need encouragement from you and an angry part may need slowing down and soothing.

 **EXPLORE**

Let's get to know one of your parts better. Choose any part you want to explore further and write it here:

When/where/how do you notice this part in your life? For example, what situations or stressors nudge this part awake?

How do you feel toward this part? Do you like it? Appreciate it? Dislike it? Hate it or reject it?

Are there any ways this part creates benefits or difficulties for you or other people? Explore and explain all the ways or give an example.

Keeping in mind that this part has good intentions, is there anything it needs from you to help it calm, heal, grow, or function differently in your life?

_____

_____

_____

*What this **PART** wants from me and for me:*

*What I want to ask, say, or offer to this **PART**:*

Nice exploring! You can always go back and repeat this exercise with other parts as the focus.

ELEVATE

Switching gears, can you remember a time when you felt just plain good? Your heart felt calm and open? Your mind felt clear, curious, and creative? Go back as far as you need to and recall this feeling as best you can. Take a few deep belly breaths and savor it for a moment before reading on.

You are more than your parts, *way more*. Your parts are like clouds that cover the sun. Your deepest self, beyond your parts, is the sun! No matter what storm clouds may cover it, your deepest core self is always there. Your internal sunshine.

According to Schwartz, there are eight qualities that define your core self: curiosity, creativity, compassion, calm, confidence, courage, clarity, and connectedness. Write about a time or times you've experienced each one. Give an example if one comes to mind.

CURIOSITY:

CREATIVITY:

COMPASSION:

CALM:

CONFIDENCE:

COURAGE:

CLARITY:

CONNECTEDNESS:

Excellent! Some people feel a combination of these qualities when they're engaged in activities such as meditation, playing or listening to music, time with animals or loved ones, dancing or doing art, cooking or baking, sports, journaling, or out in nature. What activities or practices do you have in your life that connect you with qualities of your core self?

Choose a practice or activity and write about your special relationship with it. Has it been in your life long? Do you remember the first time you realized the impact it had on you?

How often are you able to engage in that practice or activity? Is it enough for you? How might you bring more of it into your life?

Speaking of challenges, ready for your closing challenge?

Challenge: NONDOMINANT-HAND WRITING

You're trying so many new things, why not one more! Choose a tender or vulnerable part of yourself to work with for this challenge.

Write the name of that part here:

To help this part be heard, you're going to explore something called *nondominant-hand writing*. If you're right-handed, your nondominant hand (NDH) is your left hand, and if you're left-handed, your NDH is your right hand. Writing with your NDH is a tool for connecting with your vulnerable parts and helping them express themselves. (Vulnerable parts may feel young, scared, hurt, tender, neglected, abused, or abandoned.)

Think of a time (recently or more in the past) when you felt vulnerable. Make sure to pick something you feel comfortable and safe working with now. Take a deep breath and allow yourself to make an emotional connection to this part, noticing where it lives in your body. Without rushing, take a moment to connect to the energy of its mood and anything else you notice.

Now, holding a pen or pencil with your NDH, close your eyes and ask this vulnerable part if it has anything it wants you to know. When you open your eyes, let your NDH write or draw anything for the part that you're inviting into communication with you. Writing or drawing will probably feel awkward, and that's okay. This is about exploring and not about neatness.

As a final step, again making contact with the part, ask what it needs, and write the answer with your NDH. *What I need from you is:*

Thank the part for sharing, and switch your pen back to the hand you usually use for writing. What was this exercise like for you? Write about anything you noticed.

NOTE OF ENCOURAGEMENT: Many people feel that nondominant-hand writing helps them get in touch with deep feelings that are otherwise hard to access. Other benefits? Writing with your NDH can help you feel more creative and open.

PSYCH TIP: NOTICE PARTS IN THE WORLD

When you get the concept of parts, you gain more understanding about what's going on with people around you. For example, you're in an argument with someone, and they suddenly go from 0 to 100 with defensiveness and a counterattack. If you pause to observe their reaction in terms of parts, you may suspect that a vulnerable part in them has become overwhelmed and a protective part is attempting to create safety for it.

Or when you notice someone acting annoyingly full of themselves, or stubborn, or shut down, you can tap into curiosity about what this part is trying to do for the person, what its role is. At the same time, you're able to see that this part is not the entire person, which gives you the gift of valuable perspective.

Think of the people in your life and the parts of them that challenge, frustrate, or annoy the hell out of you. Consider the role this part plays in their life. Check out this example:

PERSON: Coach Natalia

TRIGGER: She has a critical, impatient part.

ROLE THIS PART PLAYS: I think she feels a lot of pressure to win. I think her critical, impatient part may be protecting her fear about our season or her fear that she's not a good enough coach.

What are some examples of people from your own life?

_____

_____

_____

This practice increases your ability to see the complexity in people, relate to them with more depth and understanding, and see their less appealing characteristics as parts of—not the whole—person.

≈ SOUL SOOTHER: COLOR YOUR SELF HAPPY!

Don't look now, but your playful child part wants a soul soother just for her. Ask your perfectionist part and inner critic to soften back, because little girls enjoy the *process* over the *product*. In other words, when you were very young and explored artistic projects, it was all about the *experience*. Inner critics and perfectionistic parts don't develop until later. Reconnect to your Playful Child by having fun coloring your Self happy with your NDH! And feel free to color way outside the lines!

Welcome to your favorites page! This is your space to write down the healthy habits that most speak to you. Come back to this page whenever you need a reminder of what you've learned.

Favorites

REFERENCES

Huberman, A. 2021. "Reduce Anxiety and Stress with the Physiological Sigh." *Huberman Lab Quantal Clip*, YouTube, April 7. https://youtu.be/rBdhqBGqiMc?si=atin09DZG 7iNEqse.

Ruden, R. A. 2010. *When the Past Is Always Present: Emotional Traumatization, Causes, and Cures.* New York: Routledge.

Schwartz, R. C. 2018. *Greater Than the Sum of Our Parts: Discovering Your True Self Through Internal Family Systems Therapy.* Audiobook. Louisville, CO: Sounds True.

LUCIE HEMMEN, PHD, is a licensed clinical psychologist in private practice in Santa Cruz, CA. For more than twenty years, she has worked with teens, their parents, and their communities in programs designed to maximize health and well-being. She is mother of two daughters, and author of *Parenting a Teen Girl*, *The Teen Girl's Survival Guide*, and *The Teen Girl's Anxiety Survival Guide*.

Publisher's Note

NEW HARBINGER PUBLICATIONS is a registered trademark of New Harbinger Publications, Inc.

New Harbinger Publications is an employee-owned company.

Instant Help
An imprint of New Harbinger Publications, Inc.
5720 Shattuck Avenue
Oakland, CA 94609
www.newharbinger.com

Cover design by Sara Christian

Interior design by Amy Shoup

Acquired by Jess O'Brien

Edited by Brady Kahn

Printed in the United States of America

26   25   24

10   9   8   7   6   5   4   3   2   1   First Printing

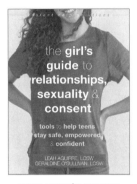
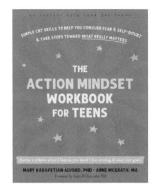

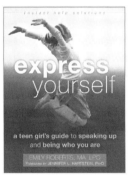